ARE YOU BROKEN?
You Can Be Restored

ARE YOU BROKEN?

You Can Be Restored

Poems and Short Stories for the Physically,
Emotionally, and Psychologically Disfigured
To Foster Hope and Change

By
Jill (Truh) Kennedy

XULON PRESS

Xulon Press
2301 Lucien Way #415
Maitland, FL 32751
407.339.4217
www.xulonpress.com

© 2018 by Jill (Truh) Kennedy

All rights reserved solely by the author. The author guarantees all contents are original and do not infringe upon the legal rights of any other person or work. No part of this book may be reproduced in any form without the permission of the author. The views expressed in this book are not necessarily those of the publisher.

Unless otherwise indicated, Scripture quotations taken from the Amplified Bible (AMP). Copyright © 1954, 1958, 1962, 1964, 1965, 1987 by The Lockman Foundation. Used by permission. All rights reserved.

Scripture quotations taken from the King James Version (KJV)–*public domain*.

Printed in the United States of America.

ISBN-13: 978-1-54565-069-1

How to Use This Book

This book is pretty much a freestyle platform and there are several ways you can use it:

1. The main story is a story of brokenness, heartache and bewilderment that will pull at your heart strings as it turns into one of the matchless love stories of all times.
2. There is a "short story" section filled with interesting real life stories of people who have overcome abuse, addiction and trauma.
3. There are poems supported by commentary
4. You may use this book as a devotional. Each commentary gives a biblical context and provokes thought.
5. Get your hands dirty in the section, where I share the therapeutic art of writing freehand poetry. "Free Writes"- try your hand at it. It is a lot of fun and has surprising results.
6. If you have a particular concern to address, the topical index will be helpful.
7. Enjoy the creative hand-drawn art by my daughter Moriah.
8. Contemplate the personal "thought questions" at the end of many of the devotionals; make notes for renewal.

You really have three books in one. You can't beat that!

Whichever way you decide to use this book, it is my hope that you will truly be blessed, and find inspiration, hope, and a motivation for change for the better.

Acknowledgements

Shirley: My mother: for her faith in me and undying love

Jeral: My son, my unsung hero

Moriah: my daughter, my counselor, my friend

Every person who has had a hand in my development throughout the years

Dedication

"Touch My Hands"

Oh Lord, Touch my Hands
Let the words from my pen, the whole world span
May they comfort and soothe,
Redirecting life's paths from rugged to smooth
Let the words to heavy hearts, speak
out loud, and
Break down barriers in a crowd
Bring down Heaven through my humble
penmanship
And create a hiding place, through my
spoken lips
When all is said and done, and the pages have
been read;
Let the sorrowing one, lay a peaceful, contented
Soul, upon his bed.

This book is dedicated to my son Jeral who was my unsung hero, finding himself in the midst of some very dark days in my life, just by being born to me. He traveled paths of uncertainty and danger but has come out on the other side stronger, and more than excited about this book. I likewise dedicate this book to my daughter Moriah, who inevitably experienced the consequence of being the daughter of one who was broken, and to one that I herald as a self-born counselor as she gave direction and comfort to me while trying to maintain a clear head and make it out alright. It is my prayer that they both, through trial and error, prayer and persistence, gain the strength and courage to stand up and make a difference. It is my goal that each of them sees the need to help others who may experience similar hardship. Ultimately, to all women and men, who have only known life as a fight for survival, and many who continue to struggle, year in and year out, day to day. And to the silent voices behind the pain of domestic, physical, emotional, and psychological abuse; those who need a voice; I certainly dedicate this work.

Table of Contents

How to Use This Book v
Acknowledgements vii
Dedication ix
Preface xv

1. My Story (From Abuse to Restoration) 1
2. Living With a Stranger 9
3. Truh Becomes a Woman 14
4. Dreams Take a Back Seat 16
5. Breaking the News 17
6. The Marriage 19
7. What of Motherhood 24
8. Tale-Tale Hints / the Birth 26
9. Abuser vs. Victim 29
10. The Missing Link 34
11. Life in a Whirlwind 39
12. Down, but Not Out 49
13. A Wilderness Experience 57
14. I've Been Kidnapped! 69
15. Redemption Draws Nigh 73
16. The Seashells Begin to Open Again 79
17. Finally, I've Been Redeemed! 81
18. Tell the world- My Appeal to You 85
19. The Color of Abuse 86
19A. The Color of Abuse 88

Devotionals and Self Help

A Masterpiece 92
Celebration 95
Silver and Gold 98
The Test 101
The Philosophy of Life 103
Never Give Up 106
That's a Sure Thing 108
My Angel 111

Short Poems

The Golden Key 116
Apology Accepted 117
Giving 120
Dry Those Tear-Filled Eyes 121
Timid Love 122
Love 123

Short Stories

Freedom IN Bondage 126
  (In The Case of Rose) 127
Run Away Eagle 131
  (Fleeing Domestic Violence) 132
Calm in the Midst of a Storm 135
  (Pounded by the Brute) 136
Fearfully and Wonderfully Made 138
  (God Saved Her Sight) 139
Tackle Your Fears 141
  (Fearful Carmen) 142
Searching For Quiet 143
  (Suicide Wins Again) 144
Race Trac: The Kidnapping 148
  (Thought Questions) 152
Good Bye My Father 155

Free Writes - Language of The Heart

    Hard Love 163
    Freedom 164
    Time 165
    Shackles 166
    Fabulosity 167
    Be Brave 168
    I Will Rise 168
    You Say 170
    A New Day 172
    Hurricane In My Heart 175
    Feet Are For Walking 178
    Never Alone 180
    I Thought You Knew 183

Index 189
Resources 195

Preface

It was a Friday afternoon in July, 1992. It had been a long day in nursing school, and I looked forward to the week-end and Sabbath rest. But I knew that I must push for more strength because I had to go and pick up my 10 month old daughter at the baby sitter before going home. As I made my last note and said goodbye to my classmates, I rushed towards the car that I was sharing with her father. I noticed that the car was parked in an ark-ward position; half in and half out of the parking space. *"Huh"*, I said to myself, *"he must have been in a real rush today"*. I didn't make anything big of it but just carried on as planned. Once, we reached home, it was made very clear to me why the car was so dis-shoveled. I walked into our 2nd floor apartment with my baby in my arms and was shocked at what I saw. It looked as though we had been robbed. But the more I looked, the more I understood, that only his things were gone. There was solemnness about the atmosphere and emptiness suddenly hit my spirit. My mate, the man who begged me to have this child with him, her father,had abandoned me, along with her. The first thoughts that flashed through my mind, was that "he made all of those promises: first and foremost: to be there; to make sure we taught her of God, to home school her, and fed her a good diet. I wanted to make a difference in her life and not just raise her carelessly. I had been a single parent before. That is never an easy job and I wanted the best for my children. It looked like something out of the movies. I could not believe what I was seeing with my own eyes. Everything he owned was gone! Clean swept! I opened the drawers that once held his under-wear and t-shirts-nothing. All of his books had been taken from the many book shelves that we had. All of his suits that hung in the closet, his shoes… everything! Not a single item, even down to his tooth brush has been left behind. I looked around for a note or something that would explain what was happening to us, but there was nothing. Not one word to explain, to comfort, to anything.

One might think this would be a good time to break down and cry and just pour out my heart with wails under the unsustainable weight of pain, but not that day. You see, I had no more tears to cry. This baby was only 10 months old and for the complete pregnancy and even for many of the few months of her young life; my eyes were reservoirs to the tears of pain and insecurity. I had to endure the sad reality of a life with a mate who was not sure of whom he was, and to one who did not want to own up to his responsibility as a parent to our child. Not to mention the child that he met me with. Who knows the damage this did to his heart and psyche. And after making promises he did not keep, he decided to simply walk away without notice. This was a classic example of total abandonment. So, I had no tears this time. I had dry sockets, and could not have mustered up a tear if my life depended on it. I had already been in a broken state for a long time. But what I did was fell to my knees, not in sorrow, but in knowing that my God was with me. I fell to my knees in prayer and embraced my Father's love and care, even in a horrific situation as this one was. I looked deeply into the eyes of that beautiful and innocent little girl, for whom I knew would never be the same. She looked at me with an impression that she knew that a huge event was happening in her life, as though she knew my heart was troubled; but she could not understand and of course could not speak to that situation. My hope, as usual, was in the Lord. This was only one of such soul stirring events in my complicated life. This difficult and horrendous space in my life was only one of many thunderous accounts at which I found very difficult to move through. You, like me, will be surprised to know why all of these life changing traumas were being hurled at me. I never understood until I finished writing this book.

But at that moment though, I took my little baby and sang songs to her, prayed and had one of the best times in worshiping God that I could remember. The Lord said that He would not give us more

Preface

than we can bear. So He held back the tears and we rested in His arms. This was only one of the many, many times that the Lord had brought me through rough patches with a smile on my face. I turned to writing, a place that helped me to heal and gave me a purpose to help others-through poetry.

My family has always asked me "When are you going to do something with the poetry and writings that has come out of you enduring hardship?" This past Thanksgiving was no different. While we sat at my dining room table for dinner, the same question came up again. My mother, my daughter, and my son all rang out in unison, "What are you going to do…where is the book?" I then sought the heart of God for the words and direction.

Well, here is that book. This book is a result of their cry, but yet, much more than that. When I began to write, God had something to prove to me that hit me like a ton of bricks. I never dreamed of how this story would turn out. Through writing this book, I have learned so many great lessons of love. I have learned that God had a purpose for me and allowed everything that I went through to lead me to Him and to prepare me for my destiny in ministering to others and to eventually walk the streets of gold. My heart was so impressed with His relentless love for me, but not only for me, but for you my dearest reader. I'll have you know that it was seven full days before I heard anything from my daughter's father… no call, no letter, nothing. Then one day he showed up out of the blue with the biggest smile on his face. He attempted to explain why he could walk away from his family. A story that would require another book all together; and even though I have forgiven him, I still have yet to wrap my head around that one. But, God restored me so that I could tell you all about His great love and care, and how He longs to do the same for you.

I write with hopes that as I have reached the light at the end of my dark tunnel, it is light enough to brighten the paths of those remaining for a time, in the darkness and abyss of pain. I invite you to take the plunge to be restored from your brokenness and find that special plan that God has for your life. I speak today to those who are or have been emotionally or psychologically disfigured. In short, those who have been hurt deeply and feel you cannot recover.

How can one be psychologically disfigured? When someone's world has been crushed by great and awful disappointments, heavy trials, his spirit shattered by the anguish of abandonment, domestic violence, divorce, human trafficking, sibling rivalry, and dysfunctional family life, resulting in the thunder of emotional pain. Surely, if you have picked up this book, it is because you are one familiar with a broken spirit. You long for comfort and perhaps a place of mental relief. You long to be able to relate to what has happened in your experience. With a hopeful heart, you have reached out and picked up this book looking for a connection. Well, I welcome you my Friend! This book was written especially with you in mind!

Perhaps you were in a relationship or marriage that ended abruptly, the relationship that you thought would last forever- "to death do you part." Maybe you've had to survive the divorce of your parents when all of your securities were met in them, the people you looked up to for everything, then, suddenly it was over. Maybe, you are fleeing a violent situation and may even still be on the run, and you've found just the perfect read for your dilemma.

Perhaps it was a close friend, even a friend you held dear for years and years, even one you'd taken for granted because you knew they'd be there no matter what. But now suddenly, they are gone. Are you the victim of a daughter's wrath? Has there been a complete sever between you and the daughter to whom you've spent so many hours in intimate relationship, thinking it was a special mother and daughter connection?

Perhaps your siblings have stepped off and determined you to be the "enemy" and you can't, for your life, figure out what happened. All you know is that you are not spoken to, by them, and are on "the outs".

No matter what type of failed relationship you are in, they all have these things in common; the pain is real, it penetrates deeply, its wound is ever present and the pain has no respecter of persons,

Preface

culture, religion, education, financial status, or age. It can happen to anyone, even you. It certainly happened to me.

This book uses a combination of my story of physical and emotional abuse, devotionals, and poetry to create something unique that seeks to help those who are physically, emotionally, or psychologically disfigured due to trauma. The book begins with the story of Rogers and Truh, (which depicts my life and the story of my first love), how our relationship turned abusive, and how we later both found God. Please be sure to note the beautiful love story of how Christ never left us alone. But He held on to us through near death encounters as the enemy of our souls tried with all his might to take from us our purpose for living. The main story is followed by devotionals and self helps that will allow you to reflect, engage, and allow for growth in your personal lives. The book is threaded throughout with original poetry. I once only wrote of darkness, but now God has restored me and shown me the light, and that is why I have written this book; to share that light with you.

My life had been a whirlwind of emotional ups and downs, but I think I finally have the answers to what God has been doing in me, in allowing the tactics of the enemy through so much pain and suffering. There are lessons I've learned that I'm glad to share with you that you might find hope and purpose in your lives and avoid some of the pit falls that I have endured. This is why it is my heart of heart's desire to speak out on this subject from my experience and about my restoration.

I believe we all go through whatever we go through so that we may not only develop moral and spiritual character, but for the sake of helping others. My book is designed for any person who has been abused or hurt, and who loves good, clean poetry, a strong love story, and would like to be engaged in original short stories of real life stuff. The audience who is spiritual in nature and encouraged by the power of God will truly be blessed with this reading. But, any person who just wishes to sit down and connect with another person who has had hardship but is finding a silver lining and is hopeful and eager to share, will find this book a treasure.

"Who Am I"

What shall I say to the people? What seed inside of me has been planted to grow a stem high as the highest steeple?
What storm has overshadowed my life and birthed an answer to inner strife?
They say all things happen for a reason. I say things happen in due season. What is the benefit of the outcome to that seemingly awful and dreadful night when it felt like I was in an uphill battle; an all day and all night, fight?
What do I say to the hearts that are hurting, seeking an answer? What modality do I use to help them come to reality? The Reality of how God works for their good – through the brunt of their pain sometimes misunderstood.
Our mere existence full of trials, we shamefully disdain as we strive to maintain
Who am I to be an instrument in the hands of an all- knowing and sovereign God? What will come out of me being discontent?
Use me God as your instrument.

Preface

 I'm glad you have come. Yes! You have experienced the groans of terrible pain that rips your heart open, stops your breath in its track. The disappointments that ravaged your very soul, leaving you to believe you've been defeated. We are so alike in our experiences. We have joys, yet misfortunes, but we don't all come back at the same rate of strength and vigor. We must be determined and ready to fight for a chance at restoration.

 This is a divine appointment, and today is the day that God has chosen to reveal to you a little more about His great and awesome plan for your life.

 The storm raged where it left off. Did you get the lesson you were meant to learn the last time the pain hit you? Well, perhaps it is the way God has chosen to teach you again.

"Life's Lessons"

Life's lessons must be learned...
Over and over again, through hardship,
Wisdom is earned
Should you miss it today,
You can rest assured
It will replay
Until you grasp the idea and, show you know it,
Know it so clear
Your future steps could be filled with fear
Life's lessons must be learned
Take time to look a bit closer
Don't miss any queues
To your survival, they could be valuable clues
Life's lessons must be learned

Preface

My heart has gone through some very tough times seeming to learn the same lessons over and over again, but the truth of the matter is that I had not learned the lesson. I had only heard it over and over again. I had not taken the time to actually take on what the experience had to teach me, but instead concentrated on what the next step would be. Well, of all the lessons in my life, the theme of a lesson that repeats over and over again; has been the most consistent one. If you don't turn on your listening ears and hear what God or the circumstance of life is trying to tell you, or what life has to offer you in a lesson; you will not move very far forward, but will only march in time. Once I finally understood that I was re-living in spaces that I had already occupied, and was not accomplishing anything, but only spinning my wheels; I started to slow down and listen, and in turn, I began to learn and progress to the places of my destiny.

These places embody the experiences that would be good for me and would be engraved in my mind for a life time.

We may feel like a day goes by with certain intricacies of its own. Sometimes of light or heavy significance, or so it may be in our minds; but you better rest assured that the lesson in that day is for eternity. What appears to be a tiny bit of information, many times holds the key to huge answers to deeper questions that may come at a later time. Have you ever thought to yourself, "I wonder why that happened to me?," or "I wonder why he/she said that?" Or even "that was stupid!" or "What did that have to do with this?"

Well, these are the times I am speaking of. These are the tiny splashes of art that completes the greater picture. These splashes of art are used sometimes in that very instance, and in other times they are put in place, over time, but they are of the same importance needed to complete the original design. All things are not expedient. In other words all things won't always happen at the same time to bring about the complete ideal. Sometimes, we must wait to see the full story come to fruition.

"A Response to Trauma"

The human body will stop at nothing to survive! Scientific America explains what happens to the brain during a trauma. "What happens when you've been through something traumatic, like a car crash or a train derailment? Often, victims don't even remember what happens. It's not because the accident was too horrible to want to remember, however, much the victim might want to piece together what happened, his brain wasn't working on making memories—it was working on survival. The same mechanisms that kept his brain sharp enough to escape immediate danger may also make it harder for both to recall the accident and to put the trauma behind him. "The normal thing is that the person doesn't remember the moment of the accident or right after," says clinical psychologist Javier Rodriguez, Escobar of trauma therapy team Group Isis in Seville. "That's because the mind and the body enter a more alert but also a more stressed state, with trade-offs that can save your life, but harms your mind's memory-making abilities. In other words, while caught up in the event itself, your brain strips down to its most basic fight-or-flight response. Oftentimes, this helps the victim think clearly enough to find an escape route-at the cost though of processes like memory- making. Adrenaline starts pumping, helping the victim to react quickly and giving him extra strength to escape his predicament." (Smithsonian.com)

In this next chapter we will begin the story of Rogers and Truh. Her name is "hurt" spelled backwards. Some of the names have been changed to protect the innocent.

Chapter 1:

My Story
(From Abuse to Restoration)

The story of Rogers and Truh:

(How the emotional and psychological dysfunction began)

Let me introduce you to an over-comer of emotional trauma. Her name is Truh, a young lady who grew up in a family of six; three siblings and both parents at home. Truh was the youngest of her siblings and found life to be fun and exciting and was a person who wanted to test her hands at many different skills. She liked the arts, creative dance, and sports, and of course, as with many of her contemporaries, grew up playing with the Barbie dolls. There were the outfits, the cars, the playhouse, and even, of course, Ken. Her past-times also included playing with her close neighbors. They grew up playing at the nearby park. Truh never really took life too seriously; she just went with the flow and found fun in picking on and teasing with her brother and sisters. Truh dreamed of becoming a Flight Attendant one day, but this would not come to fruition until much later in life. She did however, work at some pretty interesting jobs, such as being a bank teller, where she was actually robbed, but thank goodness was not hurt. Nevertheless, she was seven months pregnant at the time of the robbery. This happened much later in her young adult life. Truh was not one to be very domestic, as she had a great stay-home mother who spoiled them by preparing all the best old-fashioned, home- cooked meals and home-made desserts, which were to die for. Truh was in very good health because of the tease of the desserts as that was the tempter… "No food, no desert," so she made sure throughout her childhood to clean her plate, eating all of her vegetables too. Her favorite deserts were banana and rice pudding. Truh has a sweet tooth to this day because of it. But in reality, few people really know how to, or takes the time to prepare real home-made desserts anymore. Most cooks pour everything out of a box. Well, so much for those good -ole days. Let's get back to Truh. She was a track star at school. She ran relays and jumped hurtles as well as led the cheerleader and majorette Squads. Her team even twirled fire on special occasions. She was a good student and enjoyed learning. Truh was a real leader in her own special way; not bossy, but just had a natural talent to lead. She pretty much just lived her life in front of people, and they would follow her. She enjoyed a simple upbringing, of course had some fights with her siblings, as with all kids, but she obeyed her parents for the most part. Other than being a little goofy in breaking stuff around the house, being clumsy, she was a pretty good girl.

Speaking of being clumsy, she and her sister, were skating through the house one day, and they knew better, but how much fun is it to sneak to get away with something sometime, right? Well, Truh went gliding into the bedroom, tripped over the electric cord which apparently connected both the window fan and the television; and so out the window went the fan and bam! the television hit the floor. She got a good fussing at when her mother found out, but not in too much trouble. As you can see, Truh was an easy going young lady with big dreams, like most other girls her age and felt that she was greatly loved by her mother, as were her siblings. As for her father though, Truh had somewhat of a distant relationship with him as also, did her siblings. But they were a little older and knew more of how to maneuver his authority. He was not home much, but was out working, and they never really bonded during her childhood. But Truh had great respect for him, although she received due punishment from him when she overstepped her boundaries. A great example would be like when she disobeyed him, when he had given her explicit instructions not to eat all the candy that she had bought from the corner store one day.

When he was at work one day, Truh sneaked into the drawer where he had placed the candy after confiscating it from her. Well, just as he took the candy, she snuck it back; all ten types: now-later, lollipops, red-hots, Mary-Jane's, you name it; she had it. She then stretched out a large bundle of paper towels and poured them out with the pure, almost addictive element of joy. When just as she was ready to indulge, her dad, unexpectedly, drove up and caught her in the driveway with all that candy sprawled out on the ground. Yikes!! There was no way she could grab all of that candy up and hide it, so there she was, caught in her mess. He was not too rough in the moment, but Truh's father had a way of giving you something to remember. He told Truh that she was banned to the porch for one full month. A whole month, where she would only watch her neighborhood friends as they played with each other, but they could not come in, and she could not go out. Truh lived through that and other tough times, but nothing worse than what was in store for her. Truh would soon become the victim of the epidemic that plagues so many homes all over the world; the breakup of her family in divorce. Statistics show that 1 in 2 married couples will go through a divorce. This statistic includes Christian couples as well as non-Christian couples. The enemy of our souls has always been, and is still, out to destroy the homes. He knows that if he can destroy the homes, there goes the communities, then, there goes the Churches. He will have accomplished what he ultimately wants; to tear down God's kingdom anyway he can.

Now, that you've gotten acquainted with Truh, you have a good idea of the kind of girl she was and her surroundings, up-bringing, parents, family make-up, and can appreciate that she was a pretty average youngster. Well, take all of this into consideration as we now explore what happened to this young lady, as she experienced some unfortunate events that would change her life forever.

This poem "Seashells of My Mind" expresses how emotional trauma, even in its infant stages...led to the beginning of that phenomenon that includes a loss of long term memory. This can occur as the brain and the body makes the decision, in short order, to choose not to record the events of the moment, but chose, for the sake of Truh's life, to save her instead.

SEASHELLS OF MY MIND

Family breakdown equals family break up
Gone away to camp

Came home to a re-vamp

Daddy stopped by to say
Mom might not stay

SEASHELLS OF MY MIND

Vague memories of an empty house
Dog- abandoned there…
Place filled with his hair

SEASHELLS OF MY MIND

No one there to meet me
No one there to greet me
Mom must have fled the scene
Doors unlocked, holes in the screen

SEASHELLS OF MY MIND

Must have hurt bad
Blanked it out of my mind
don't remember cry'n
Can't reach back for details
Counseling only unlocked the end tales

SEASHELLS OF MY MIND

My Story

This is Truh's account of what happened as this string of events started with the break- down of her family:

"I was at Summer Pre-College Camp when I received an un-expected visit from my father. When I looked up and saw him, I immediately cringed because he was like a foreign object to me. I was not so sure of what to do with it, the visit I mean. He said, very matter-of-factly…"Your mother and I will be getting a divorce… who do you want to stay with?" Wow! This was, first of all, such a surprise, as I never had any idea, that anything was wrong. You see my parents had never fought in the presence of me and my siblings. At least, I don't recall them having even the least argument let alone a physical fight. Oh, there was one time, when they began to argue, but I can remember my father saying to my mother, who started the conversation…"Don't you see the kids?" and then the conversation ended, just as quickly as it started.

Ok, so his entrance onto the campus to talk with me was an abrupt surprise, seemingly like out of nowhere. Then the way he just laid it all out there hit me like a ton of bricks. *"Hey"*, I thought… *"Please, give me time to absorb the first part." "You are divorcing." "What happened?" " Was it something I did?" " Who else knows?" " When is all of this going to take place? What will happen to me? How is my mother and what is she thinking about all of this? Why didn't she come to see me?"* These and a thousand other questions went through my mind, as he stood, what felt like towering over me; as I sat on the steps below. My first response came as I quickly tried my best to assess the damage and find a hiding place for my wounded heart. I quickly, without thinking things through, told him, "I'll stay at home," in response to the question: "Do you want to go with her, or stay with me?"

Where was she even going? Talk about a lot of information with a lot of holes in it! Hopefully he stayed with me for questions and some form of comfort. But from what little I can remember, it seemed like he just turned and walked away as quickly as he showed up, leaving my head spinning in space. I knew he meant well, but that was just his way, and boy did it sting. I buried this information in my heart and carried it inside for all of the remaining weeks that I attended my wonderful Pre-College Program which, by the way, was the best experience of my life! I was learning and growing in a college setting, sparking a sense of what I wanted to become. I was figuring out what my next steps in life would be; a very critical place in my development. With retrospect, I can understand why this news of my parent's divorce did so much damage to my psyche.

Anyway, the days that followed went as planned with lots of fun, and excitement. I really cannot remember at this time, but I am sure I probably tossed that information around in my head a couple of times before I dismissed it until it was time to face the music, several weeks later."

Follow Truh as she has finally completed camp and returns home. She has not spoken to anyone about this incident from that point until her arrival at home.

Truh arrived at home with a friend, whose name cannot be recalled at this time, but it appeared that they were well acquainted. They entered through the front porch screen door. This is the same porch that was a place of very familiar memories, mostly very fun, and others, not so fun. The place where her growing up had been spent with family and friends. Her mind flashed back to that long summer punishment after stealing the candy her father told her not to eat. She looked around and noticed all the changes that had taken place in such a short amount of time. The flower pots all had dead plants, where great life was once in each of them when her mother was there. She had taken for granted the beauty that they brought to that loving environment. But now that they were all dead, their appearance was no longer taken for granted. The yellow brownish leaves up against the dry dirt, glared at her in pity. She wished that she could only return to that once lively space in time again. There were holes in the screen door, something her mother would never have stood for. But since it appeared that no one was home, she stuck her hand through the hole and unlocked the screen to let her and her friend inside. After successfully gaining entrance into the porch, the next challenge would be to enter the bedroom that she shared with her sisters. Truh heard a loud and unfamiliar bark coming from the behind that door. After knocking again and still no answer, although somewhat frightened, she and her friend got up enough courage to finally open the door. To their shock, a larger than life sized, Collie looked them square in the eyes. Unassuming, he stood in a circle of his summer shed hair. He was silently glaring at them as they whispered to each other, *"should we go in? Wonder if he will bite?"* and they took the chance to yell out *"Is anybody home?"* There was no reply, but the dog, started toward the door when "SLAM!" they closed the door and ran, only to return and try it again and again.

After perhaps an hour, they came to the conclusion that he would not bite, and they slowly entered the house. Once they were inside, the Collie sniffed them and rendered them harmless as well. They traveled through the house looking for signs of family members or some indication of what to expect next. The atmosphere was uncanny, so quiet, and somber. Truh and her friend had come from an outright party of a Summer-camp, to an empty house with no one there to welcome her back or to even let her know what to do. Reality hit home for Truh. She remembered the brief talk she had with her dad on the college campus. Disbelief now turned into denial, and the darkness of pain shocked Truh to her very core. It seemed to cover her imagination. And what seemed like "seashells of her mind" began to lock the doors and block the entrances to the corridors that would lead to spaces of innocent exploration in her young life. The free spirited, enchanting, trusting, fun-loving, daring young girl began a metamorphosis. She began to change into a person to whom she would not know for many years to come. Not realizing the danger that was now set in motion by her innocent forward move; Truh continued to travel through what seemed like an abandoned ship-wreck. By taking the next step to uncover more of this sad, revelation, of what appeared to be a deserted family, she placed herself in that metamorphic state.

Truh, at that moment, began the walk from a carefree, spirited lifestyle into a darker world of overprotection, anger, depression, insecurity, and never feeling the safety she once felt.

It has been said, that what happens in the formative years of a child's life will be the deciding factors used to form who that child will become; whether positive or negative. Truh's mind began to block out all of the details of her parent's divorce and carried on with a strong willed idealistic way of dealing with her pain.

Upon walking through that door on that momentous day, seeds of change that would affect forever, how she loved, lived, would deal with pain, and who she would pay homage to, would be planted. The betrayal of friendships, the secret hatred for those she thought she loved and cared for, the ones she thought cared for and loved her, would have deep roots and would not be discovered and removed for many years.

The veil of protection clouded her psyche and for decades, the truth of why she acted and thought the way she did, why she had certain fears, why the insecurities and more, will be lost until the seashells are opened again. The opening of the seashells of Truh's mind (meaning psychotherapy) would begin the discovery of how Truh's mind worked to defend her. How Truh rediscovered her natural self-worth after many decades of allowing emotional, psychological, and physical abuse to play key roles in her existence, will be disclosed in chapters ahead.

Chapter 2:

"Living With a Stranger"

The initial shock of the onset of the separation and divorce had ended. Truh's mother, the one who would hold the family together with love, creativity, fun, baking, conversation, and celebration during the holiday seasons, and just good ole fashion family life, would be, for now, alien. Her absence would be felt deeply, but the pain of the reality of it all would keep Truh from experiencing her sincere feelings and bringing about a change. The days would come and go, filled with the mystery of "why" and "how", and, of course, the question of "was it my fault?" Truh's mind switched to a safety mode and blocked out the trauma to create a safe place for continued growth and development. She made her best attempts to move forward in life, nevertheless, without dealing with this dilemma.

Now, not only had Truh's mother left, but her last sibling left at home had also found it a good time to begin her independence. This was totally against Truh's all-out wails for her to stay. Therefore, a new world of silence and fear of the unknown had begun.

Remembering that Truh's father was a workaholic and had now begun to immerse himself more and more in his work, does not help the situation. I'm sure however, he had bigger struggles, than ever, since losing his wife of many years. Even so, her father put forth every effort to spend more time teaching Truh important lessons for life. These practical lessons such as how to write out checks and how to pay bills would never be forgotten. Truh found herself having flash backs of them sitting at their kitchen table as she learned how to handle the business of life every time she pays her bills, even to this day. There would be times when they would go out for a bite to eat and to play bingo with his friends. At home though, the saying "I could hear a pin drop," applied to their life as the mother's vibrant personality was no longer alive there. Now that the dust had settled from all of the immediate confusion, Truh came to realize that she did not really know her father at all. All of the years in this family, her mother was the star of the show, the one who was there and would make things happen as far as the things a child would remember; the fun stuff, the things that makes life stimulating and exciting. Of, course,her father would be given credit for financially supporting the family so that the "sparkle" could happen, but as children who cares about that?

Now, Truh lived with a stranger, at least, that is how it felt to her with such a sudden adjustment.

Many nights Truh's father would call her to the table as he made telephone calls to his friends. Truh would cringe at the sound of being called by him although she would come as quickly as she could with a sweet disposition, but screaming on the inside. He would say to his friends on the phone, "oh yes, me and my lovely daughter are sitting here sharing and talking together." In Truh's mind, she would hope to be released from what seemed to her like a prison. Not that her father was mean, but only because the foundation had not been laid for communication and she was extremely shy and not used to him. How would you like to, all of a sudden, be sent to live with a person, parent or not, who you don't really know; especially at the same time you are losing a special person in your life that you do know?

With her sweet smile, she simply carried on with the flow and would quickly, like lightening, run to her room once the "talk" was over. Let's just say, she was saved by the bell when he would continue to get calls from his friends. Truh would go to her room and pretend to be reading a book just to keep an image of being "ok" if her father should ask her what she was doing; which he often did.

Truh was not, however, the only one going through some major changes here. He must also have been making jumps and strides to keep it together. He was now living in spaces he had never occupied.

"Living With a Stranger"

When Truh's father would leave for work or be out of the home for any reason, this was her time to be free and come out of her shell. Her love for music and dancing would lure her to the formal living room where the stereo and albums were kept. There was a large picture window to keep track of when he might show up, as his whereabouts were sometimes unpredictable. Maybe he was as unsure of how to manage a young girl who he had just inherited full time as much as she was unsure of being the inherited one.

She would come alive, dancing and playing music by Michael Jackson and Al Green and talking on the phone. This would surely be a surprise to him because he never knew she was a party hog in his absence. Then, the minute he was spotted coming up the driveway, off went the music with her heart beating one thousand beats a minute. She would run back to her room to the normal isolation and pretend to read again. Whew! Again, she would hear, her name being called..."Truh...how are you my daughter?" And the cycle would start all over again. The only thing Truh could think of was the fact that she now lived with the man whom she barely knew when her siblings were there. He would come home every day with a frown on his face, and often complained about what was not done, "Who left the bike in the driveway? Who turned up the heat so high?" She and all of her siblings would take off running in all different directions. But now, there were no siblings there with her, and nowhere to run. As a little girl she was scared to death of her father, but it was no big deal because she never had to face him alone; but what about now?

Truh's mother would stay in touch though the conversations were short and the relationship somewhat strained. Truh kept her true feelings about life inside and only exchanged small talk. Truh would assure her mother that she was "just fine." She no longer allowed her mother to get as close as they used to be, but spoke, instead, to her high school sweetheart, in whom she confided everything. This went on for several months. To look from the outside one would think, "*Well, how great an adjustment Truh is making." She seemed to be doing just fine.*" However, going back to the seashells of Truh's mind's experience, it was not that at all. Truh, had simply closed off that chapter of her life and switched on to a more pleasant space where she felt self-worth, loved and safe in her new relationship with her friend Rogers.

Truh continued this unrelenting relationship with her sweetheart Rogers; who was actually in the midst of his own family disruption. Rogers's mother and sibling had recently moved away. He chose, however, to remain in the apartment they had as a family. Now Rogers and Truh were both turning to each other for comfort and assurance which would eventually turn into the worse co-dependent situation ever. She often sat with him on the front porch, (Yes, that same front porch; if only walls could talk.) and have long talks about life. Truh asked Rogers the hard questions as if he would know the answers. He was her same age and had his own baggage. Truh was told by Rogers many, many years later, that she once, asked him, "How could my mother leave her little girl?" Truh, of course could not remember this and since many years had passed. At that point, she and her mother were the best of friends as the story will eventually unfold.

2 ½ years later: Truh is now 17 years old

The time was surely moving, and True had allowed life to be busy with school and extracurricular activities. She had always been pretty popular in school and she was now the head of the majorette squad and spending many hours creating and planning new routines to perform during football season. Track had also been one of her favorite sports. She placed second in the hurdles and in the long jump, and her albums were filled with pictures of the accomplishments she made in sports as well as being the newspaper editor, Homecoming Queen, and enjoying all sorts of fun activities. But, her personal life had been shut away inside. Truh continued to live in silence with the man she considered a stranger. No one really knew what was happening; I mean really happening with her at home. Truh looked and seemed so happy that the initial and constant concern from her teachers has quieted down. They all assumed that all was well, even Truh thought so. Nevertheless, she had only gone and left behind, temporarily, the real issues that would fester and come to a head as they manifested in ways not imagined.

Truh held deep secrets and expressed only these secrets of the heart with the only one she felt cared for her- Rogers. Real life, grown up issues,were about to take place as Truh's relationship with Rogers grew stronger.

They were so close that even her father would make the remark, "If you see one, you see the other." This must have somehow been a relief for Truh's father in having her occupied with her boyfriend. I'm sure, he saw her smile more and gave the false hope that she was alright." He did not realize that this was not a good thing, but co-dependency was developing between young hearts and minds. Well, she was treading thin ice and following the heart that would soon be tricked and broken along with his.

Chapter 3:

"Truh Becomes a Woman"

On a hot summer night, the scene took place in a community called Glory Manner; a place known as "the capital of the ghetto". This place was the home of prostitutes, pimps, and the drug abuse. The question may be asked, what would any well-raised, respectable, young lady be doing there? The answer is: looking for love in all the wrong places. As the saying goes and the old question is raised, "Why do good girls like bad boys?" You see, Truh had found this place to be a home away from home because her boyfriend Rogers was born and raised in these low income apartments. But now that his family had picked up and moved away, he had set up shop in their old apartment. Truh was intrigued by the idea that her boyfriend was man enough to work and took care of business on his own. Perhaps she felt that if he could do that for himself, then maybe he would be well able to take care of her.

The evening, I'm sure, had been well-planned by Rogers, who looked forward to showing Truh the ropes. She had visited so many times before but he hoped and imagined that this time would be very special, because at this point in their relationship, he found himself in love with his high school sweetheart. He was ready to take on the challenge of where this next step would lead.

The lights were dimmed, and the melodies of Al Jarreau played in the background as Rogers lit incense that would carry the romance of young love for the remainder of the evening. Truh, with all of the innocence of youth, looked to Rogers for total guidance, step-by-step, as he gently led her. He took care to cover all bases to ensure protection from her new-found love. Rogers managed to convince Truth that all would be okay. He slowly, carefully, and gently embraced her. Truh's eyes filled with tears of innocence and her body screamed with splendor as the two youthful, vibrant, lavishly stimulated bonds connected one to another. The exhilarating exchange of passion and young love sent an emotional charge to change forever the meaning of where their friendship stood. They were never to be only friends, but lovers for life. The night continued as Rogers held, cuddled, and reassured his baby. The baby, whose cry, only he alone would be able to comfort and console; had just been born. They had yet to realize what had really happened that night. Yes, they had now become one, but she had also bound herself to another in an emotional bonding that would always feel the excruciating pain of divorce, should, for any reason, there be a separation between them. The love of her father, her brother, and her uncles, would become second place in her life. These affections would now be sought after in Rogers. He would feel the burden of supplying for Truh all the important roles those male family members should have played, as he had so isolated Truh from the world she once knew. In one night of passion, she had gone from an innocent girl with a shattered heart, to a woman who thought herself in love, and a slave to emotional codependence. Would this "love" stand the test of time?

Chapter 4:

"Dreams Take a Back Seat"

*F*or a couple of years, living in a dream world seemed to the young couple to be grown-up and secure. Minor trials that Truh and Rogers thought their love would surely conquer, were their only roadblocks.

While entrenched with the full force of Rogers's influence at this time, Truh thought the world of him. Time passed and they became more comfortable with their intimate involvement. Truh was still trusting Rogers's advice and depending on his leadership while her father worked long hours. She was thoroughly convinced that Rogers's cry against her career choice of becoming a flight attendant was his true expression of love. Rogers played a major role in her emotions and he reminded her of how he had been there for her and would never leave her *"like her Mama did."* While, for the emotionally stable, this cry would be the sign of a red flag, but for the emotionally disfigured this cry of codependence and control sounded like the sincere words of love and endearment.

Truth's career plans became second to marriage and a baby boy to be born in February. This would be three months sooner than they had planned to wed the following April.

With the news of being pregnant, Truh felt totally excited as she was so in love and head over heels with Rogers. She could only think of this creation to be what she saw when she looked at him; the father to be and the love of her soul. They both gladly looked forward to that little bundle of joy that could only bring happiness and bonding to their union. But there was a shadow over their heads… How would they break the news to Truh's dad?

Chapter 5:

"Breaking the News"

The day had come, when the old man must come to know what he might already have suspected. Truh and Rogers had planned for days upon days, their strategy for letting Truh's father know that he was about to become a grandfather and moreover, that his little girl was about to marry and move out.

Heading down what had always seemed like the divided zones of safety and the zones of terror, they walked the long hall to her father's bedroom. This was the hall that she and her siblings fearfully maneuvered whenever they needed to talk to their father about important matters. It was made of old oak wood with cracks and weakened points, which made it impossible to walk on without being heard. They did the same thing she and her siblings used to do. Before they took the leap of faith and walked down the hall as it cracked and creaked in approaching her father's room, they counted to 10, over and over again. After several attempts, they finally got up the courage to first yell his name down the hall; the name which they had called him (Lee) all during their childhood. This was because her grandmother, for some time, lived with the family, and the children picked up the habit of calling their parents what the grandparents called them, by their first names. The answer came back a familiar "yeah?" Truh yelled back: "Rogers and I would like to come and talk to you."

"Okay, "Come on back," he answered.

Truh went ahead and Rogers waited at the end of the hall. Nevertheless, both hearts were beating as one army of drums. They were both filled with terror to now have to approach a man that neither of them really knew; with the news that could worsen an already awkward situation. The news that will, on one hand, bring a great sense of relief to the young couple; while on the other, hand could split the heart of an unsuspecting father. The door was closed as Truh approached her father's room. Once inside, the news was given as quickly and as harmlessly as possible while Rogers awaited a call on the other side of the door. Immediately, he was summoned to come in. Their hearts began again, to beat as one, as they held each other emotionally through eye contact and the intuitive instinct that they were there for each other. The words of sarcasm were spoken by her father: "Oh, yeah, when you live like grown people, you get what grown people get... And like I've always told you, if you get yourself a baby, you take care of it."

Truh's reply was a simple "okay". Only vague memories were held of what Rogers had to say as he was reminded of his less than adult status.

Once the news was delivered, the two flew out of the house with such fire and with a great sense of relief. The burden has been lifted, but, unbeknownst to Truh, this news would nearly break her father's heart. Off to Six Flags they went, as two young children seeking a place of explosion and freedom.

Now the next and huge task of marriage along with motherhood, which Truh knew absolutely nothing about, would begin. This new phase of their lives would be the start of an emotional roller coaster that would prove more difficult, all together, than any they would ride that day at Six Flags.

Chapter 6:

"The Marriage"

Unfortunately, their marriage took place before a Judge in a courtroom. The cart was placed before the horse, so now, one must catch up. In doing so; deny some of the sweeter delicacies that mature, well-planned individuals enjoy. Such as a wedding in a church, the long wedding gown which every young girl dreams of. Most girls have planned out every single detail, from the wedding colors, to the lace, to how it will match the veil. And, of course, the tuxedo for the groom; not to mention the three-tiered cake and the ride off into the sunset while the entire wedding party and the parents look on with pride and blissful hope for the couple to enjoy their honey moon, as a start to a great and fulfilling life together.

Well, Rogers and Truh weren't off to the best start. But of course, "love" would see them through… or so they thought. Their first several months felt like a wonderful dream of grownups playing house with no one around to set rules and tell them what to do. Having moved emotionally and physically away from any restraint or even memory of the pain of their past, they forged ahead. Rogers had been removed from separation anxiety that he experienced as his whole family left him behind when they moved away to another state. His pain was blinded by the responsibility that Truh placed on him as she leaned on him for everything that her family could have delivered. They were now grossly blinded by their infatuation and young love for one another. "On top of the world", they thought, but everything that goes up, must come down.

Their first Christmas as a married couple would prove to be quite a memorable event.

Christmas was fast approaching. The holiday sales were advertised on every radio and television channel. People scurried to post-Thanksgiving and pre-Christmas shopping sprees. The traditions of lights and Christmas trees could be seen for miles around. For Truh and Rogers, this meant the anxiety of being like "The Jones's". Yet they had a financial struggle because she was now about 7 ½ months pregnant. Truh was working as a bank teller and Rogers worked hard and long hours as a mechanic technician for a large auto part company in the city. These jobs were fine when they had fewer responsibilities. But now, especially with the baby on the way the budget was tight. The budget was so tight, that they could not even afford a Christmas tree for their townhouse apartment. This was the home that Truh followed Rogers to after making that big step in marriage. Rogers had seen fit to move away from that ghetto scene he grew up in. This was the same place that Rogers invited Truh to come to when he had many parties with friends that they both knew and loved. This was the same townhouse that was the host of an offensive encounter with ghetto girls who fought to keep Rogers a single man by coming by and threatening Truh's safety. This same place would eventually be the home of their firstborn.

They did all they could to make the holiday season one of happiness and peace; yet the reality of the struggle of lives under pressure would prove to be a hardship that mature love would have a difficult time handling, let alone, what Truh and Rogers's young love could handle. Even a love they thought would endure anything.

After realizing they would not be able to afford a store-bought Christmas tree, they went hand-in-hand across the street from their townhouse to a wooded lot to find a tree that they could call their own. After traveling back and forth through the woods, they decided on a scrawny four-foot twig. This was the best they could find. Laughter echoed throughout the woods as they got a kick out of how "broke "they were, but they embraced each other as Rogers promised Truh that things will only get better for them in time. The love and the commitment of young sweethearts maintained that strong bond and they brought the little pitiful looking tree home and decorated it with the lights they had. This memory of their first

"The Marriage"

Christmas tree as a newly, married couple, would never be forgotten. As a matter of fact, that experience would be a stronghold for when times would get even harder.

Rogers, being a young man with great pride, however, had not only internalized this Christmas experience, as a time to remember in sweet and innocent love; but for him, it remained stamped and etched in his mind as a failure. He was always full of promises to Truh and he wanted the best for her but he never imagined that their commitment in marriage would be such a big responsibility. So, as he worked day by day, the memory of that walk to the woods became a shameful letdown for him. As it was Rogers's custom, he'd have a beer and hang out for a few hours with his guy friends to shake off the pressure. Truh, of course, still looked up to Rogers and with understanding and respect for what he had gone through in recent months. Without his family there to support him, she gave him all the support he needed; so she thought. Christmas came and went, and they made it through with great support of each other. There were also friends that Truh had come to know through Rogers who also were there for support and fellowship. Truh was now becoming quite the antisocial personality, as she had very few friends that she had established.(Note, that the bubbly, outgoing, personality had begun to change) Even though in high school, where she and Rogers both attended, Truh had been very outgoing, leader of the majorette squad, cheerleader Captain, track and field superstar etc. She could never have made it to be the Homecoming Queen with an antisocial personality, so something was definitely going wrong.) Let's remember that she had left all of her high school friends and acquaintances back in that world and had now had come to attach herself to whom she wished to be with- Rogers. (This is a very practical characteristic of the domestic abusers. They, many times, isolate their victim from their family and friends so that their manipulation and control will be seen by their victims, as love. Sometimes the abuser is aware of their actions and many times they are not.) Perhaps with Truh's experience with her parent's divorce, the pain of it all made it necessary to not only leave that moment in time behind, but also everything and everyone who was a part of that moment, and the embarrassment it presented. Truh now latched on to what she assumed was a world of safety – Rogers's world. He was, after all, the one who was there for her in her dark times of hurt and loneliness. How easily we remove ourselves from places of pain and emotional trauma. However, too many times we place a lack of importance in trying to rectify what went wrong in those places in our lives. Yet the psyche, the emotional space, the need for growth, all must be set in positive motion. The right direction must be sought, before we may safely move forward in a healthy stride. As you will see, this will not happen in the experience of Truh; only to her down fall.

Having moved from that place in her life... the place that determined who she would become, the place of happiness and support through sad times, the place where her roots and family and childhood friends were, the place of early educational development and close associations with teachers and people who could prove to be special building blocks for her life were. Not realizing what she was doing, Truh had left all-of-this behind. In heart, in physical realm, in, what might have been hopes for the future, even her emotions, were in every sense of the words "left behind". In other words Truh had left herself behind. She had, because of that awful pain of the divorce of her parents, decided to leave who she was, what she thought she stood for, all of her promises and dreams, behind, in hopes for a new life.

As the story continues, focus on how Truh deals with this newness of character. See how she deals with the challenges before her, and how, for so long, she doesn't realize that she must go again to pick up the pieces of her shattered life. She must re-channel her feelings and she must get help to fix what is broken before moving forward.

"The Marriage"

.... We may run, we may hide
but there is no true hiding place
we must, with hope, return to a familiar space,
uncover the wrongs done to us,
and decide to look at them face-to-face
Forgive and express grace.
But not until this is done,
will there be success climbing up of the
ladder's wrung,
Or make any sense or free us from the mold
of defense,
return now to your familiar space
all the pain, to dispense.

Chapter 7:
"What of Motherhood"

The holidays had passed and the couple focused on the soon birth of their baby. The pregnancy had been healthy and a lot of fun for Truh. Only two unwelcomed experiences were recorded… One day on the bus, Truh was standing in the midst of a crowd, where more men were sitting than women, when she felt a flush of faintness and began to sweat profusely. After trying to maintain her composure, she finally asked the man sitting directly in front of her big belly, "May I please have your seat?" "I'm not feeling well." She was so disgusted to have to ask the question and figured the offer to have his seat would come freely with her belly right in his face. Unfortunately, he got up with hesitancy, but she was able to sit before she fainted. Chivalry was certainly dead on that ride home, but not only on the bus ride. At home, Rogers had begun to drink and do drugs a lot more when he became stressed. In the midst of all of the changes, she and Rogers had an argument during which Rogers pushed Truh around and even spit in her face; keep in mind she was pregnant with his child.

Otherwise, Truh ate as many pancakes, as often as she could, gained all the weight she felt like, and drove Rogers crazy wearing this certain pair of slippery sandals that seemed to be dangerous. But Truh felt in her heart that she could master them and would not hurt herself.

(The signs of abusive behavior were becoming more and more apparent. Was Truh taking these actions seriously?) For so many, the acts of abuse appear to be such a daily normal that unless they are beat, pushed around, and mistreated, they don't feel they are truly loved. This is such a sad commentary.

By the time Truh was well-established in her pregnancy, she allowed her mother to make great strides in becoming a regular part of her life again. However, this closer connection between mother and daughter caused some friction for Rogers. He was sometimes upset when her Mom, who was absent during that huge struggle surrounding the divorce. He questioned how she could now step on the scene and offer so much advice. Rogers was beginning to feel the competition between them. This was a possible threat to his strategy, which was probably not really understood, even by him. This strategy was to isolate Truh in order to maintain his "hero" status in her life. Nevertheless Mom came over to help decorate and paint and get all things ready for the new arrival. The nursery was a nice mild blue, just perfect for a baby boy. All of the baby gifts that were given to Truh at her shower were placed strategically in the nursery. Truh would, on several occasions, go in to adore the readied nursery and the tiny outfits hanging in the closet. She could only imagine what their baby would bring to their lives. By this time, stress was creeping up on Rogers and he had more and more occasions when he needed a beer or a smoke and to hang out with the boys. Occasional drinking and smoking was very much a part of Rogers and Truh's lifestyle prior to the baby. However, we will come to see that Rogers was having a love affair, not only with Truh, but with something that later proved to be too strong for him to break without intervention.

Chapter 8:

"Tale-Tale Hints / the Birth"

*I*t seemed that many occasions presented themselves for Rogers to become overburdened and even out of control. Once during Truh's pregnancy Rogers shoved her around, pushed her down. and kicked her in her shin after an argument of sorts. Truh felt a sense of insecurity in Rogers and a very hostile and a jealous spirit, which was not new, but worsening. The financial burdens were mounting, and it seemed there was no escape. The one good thing though, was that the medical insurance coverage came in the nick of time, just one day before their baby would be born. That relieved a lot of pressure, but only for a while. The real pressure wasn't linked to finances alone, but the remedy that Rogers chose to relieve the pressure had become a noose around his neck. Neither of them would figure this out for quite some time.

Finally, it was the moment of promise; a baby boy was born! It was happily uneventful, other than Rogers getting overly excited when Truh told him she was in labor. He leapt to his feet from sleeping, changed his clothes at least four times, before he was ready to go to the hospital. Once arriving at the hospital, Truh was told that she had dilated but was not quite ready for the delivery. She was given the task of walking up and down the hospital halls. Rogers was attentive and by her side. There was a certain nurse who took special care to make sure Truh was treated with great kindness and patience. She sat down to explain to Truh, as a mother would, all of what was going on with her baby now that she was in active labor. The nurse was careful to explain the baby's location in the uterus, the expansion of and squeezing of the uterine muscles on the baby and hence the reason for so much pain. This was a moment in time that Truh would never forget. For that moment, she was made to feel as though she was the only patient in that hospital and that nurse was hired specifically for the delivery of her baby. These times in ones lives are known as critical points and are marked for negative or positive experiences for each of us. For Truh, this was a remarkable and awesome show of compassion from one human being to another. Even though this nurse was only doing her job, she showed the special kindness and consideration that would save a damaged young woman for such a time as that. This nurse had no idea of Truh's history and that she was already in the midst of domestic violence, at the iceberg's tip, but she did well to treat her as though she did know.

During the long, 18-hour labor process, Truh, found she was getting pretty sick of Rogers and the other nurse, who somehow, got into a conversation about algebra, of all things. Truh hated math! The pain would come and go, and it seemed that when the contractions were at their height, Rogers and the nurse would talk the deepest on and on about algebra… until Truh finally shouted out: "Will you please shut up talking about algebra!?"

The labor was strong, but the doctor's had to use forceps to pull the baby through. Truh remembered hearing the cracks of his skull as he was being pulled out. What an awful sound for a young, first time mother to hear, but the doctors made sure all was well. The doctor informed her that this was a common procedure.

When, finally, at 2:12 p.m. a little handsome boy was born. The doctors in kidding called him, "big head," but they said he had such strong neck support. Well, the birth was successful and now Rogers and Truh were proud parents of a 7lb 61/2 oz. baby boy.

After the baby was born, the doctor laid him gently onto Truh's chest. At that moment, Truh had no idea of how to be a mother. She simply looked at that warm, needy little body for a moment, then looked into Rogers's eyes and he knew to take over from there. She could feel the pressure of being a mom creeping up already.

Back in those days, the labor and delivery process was a long experience where the mothers and babies stayed in the hospital for 4-5 days. Truh took advantage of this time to recover and begin to prepare for motherhood.

She was glad that Rogers was there and could pick up where she left off with his loving personality, always seeming to do the trick. Rogers and baby found themselves the best of buddies right from the start, which actually bloomed into an inseparable relationship.

Whew! For Truh, however, this would be a big feat, and a lesson on love, as this was not her best area, but she always knew she could look to Rogers for help. She rested and enjoyed watching the baby and daddy in motion and she would catch up on her rest when the nurse would come to take him back to the nursery; until the day came when she and her little bundle would leave for home. Once they arrived safely at home, new baby in hand, she didn't know what to do first, so she thought, *I'll turn on the mobile that we got at the shower…That'll keep him, at least, until I figure out my next move.* Truh placed a tiny marsh mellow on her nose-all in fun- and she sat herself down in front of the aquarium to just think for a minute.

Chapter 9:

Abuser vs. Victim

Rogers and Truh began their lives as a young couple with real responsibilities and they now have a new bundle of joy to care for. The pressure began to build as Rogers faced more and more financial struggles. They began to realize that they both needed more than what they were equipped with. They required much more support than they had between just each other and their friends. Truh's mother had remained in the picture and the relationship was picking up with great strides, which also set off the anger and insecurities in Rogers. He felt he had been her all and all and that he was losing his grip on her as her mother had become more a part of Truh's life. Rogers began to use drugs more frequently and his drinking was getting out of hand.

The enemy of our souls would play a large role in both Rogers and Truh's life for several years to come, as he would entice them in their codependency and addictions. He would make sure they misunderstood the magnitude of the situation they were in. Rogers would miss his parents, and family, but would not own up to it. His pride caused him to deny asking for help but to press forward to be all that he could be in his own strength. Day after day he worked his job and attempted to build a good home for his family. All while allowing the enemy to nearly take the life of his first love by his own hands with each outburst of anger and abusive behavior. They struggled through a life that they designed when they made the choice to walk away from what they knew. All that they knew to be life: their families, broken as they were, friends and familiar surroundings; they left behind. Rogers continued with his pacifier in alcohol and drugs that only would pacify for a time. His temper got the best of him and, he was totally overrun with his jealous streak that kept Truh on pins and needles. He would not allow anyone to even look at her. She got a beating or yelled at if a man looked her way; but what could she do about what another person does with their own eyes? This just showed the cowardliness and immaturity in him, as he knew he couldn't do anything to them, but he could cowardly take it out on her.

Truh's mother was now a very big part of her life and they got along wonderfully. They moved past the pain of the divorce, but now Truh's mother had come to know that Rogers had a problem with his anger. One day, just out of the blue, when Truh was home talking on the phone with her mother; Rogers came home. Before he could get in the door good, he zoned in on Truh and immediately wanted to know who she was talking too. With his eyes bulging, and a frowned up face, he demanding of her: "Who you talking too?" "My mom" said Truh. "I don't think so" said Rogers as he pulled the phone cord out of the wall and threw it to the floor. It was obvious that Rogers had been drinking and was already under the command of the poison that he loved so. Truh knew that that was going to be one of those nights so she attempted to get a few things and leave the house, when Rogers jumped up in her face and accused her of leaving to go and see another man. No amount of convincing would get him off of her back and he continued to yell at her up close in her face; while he yanked her by her pony tail. "I know that man was on the phone and you think you gonna go and run to him now, don't ya!" said Rogers. Truh almost vomited by the lethal smell of his mouth. "There is no other man", said Truh. The more she tried to tell him the truth, the more the liquor would talk, until he began to push her around, grabbing her by the throat and getting in her face and threatened to kill her if she had another man. The thing about Truh, by now, is that she had gotten tired of being pushed around, so whenever, Rogers would want to put his hands on her; she did not back down, and this, like so many other instances, turned into an all-out fist fight. Chairs were thrown, dishes were broken, and blood and tears were mixed. Unfortunately sometimes these fights would be in the presence of their little boy.

It was, however, not understood if Truh's mother knew whether or not he had a drinking habit and drug addiction, but nevertheless, she was quite aware that there was abuse and urged Truh to leave that situation less there should be harm to her and their little boy who happened to love his father with the greatest love. Interestingly enough, Rogers, even though an addict and alcoholic, was surprisingly a good father. Outside of these episodes when he was in a drunken stupor, he was very attentive and loving and really wanted the best for his child but would not accept the fact that he, himself, was broken.

It is not until one realizes that he/she has a problem, that he/she will be able to do anything about it. Rogers was just, in fact, acting out Proverbs 20:1 "Wine is a mocker and beer a brawler, whoever is led astray by them is not wise." He is now in the clenching grip of that other lover in his life.

His pride was bigger than life and there was no one to convince him of the fact that he needed an outside source to help him. Rogers's father, who was an alcoholic, was not seen in his life again since the time when Truh got to meet him at the beginning of their relationship. (Sadly he was sprawled out on the concrete as he hung on to a pole right in the midst of a busy city intersection; unaware of who Rogers was, let alone the girl he was introducing as his girlfriend.) His addictive presence, which could have been a constant reminder of the problem with alcoholism, was not there to help them.

The years passed as they lived from paycheck to paycheck and did their best in raising their son. They continued to have parties, music blaring, drinking and smoking as their norm. They were so innocent to the dangers of their lifestyle which was heading in the wrong direction. There would be spats from time to time, usually after Rogers had a few drinks, but even if he did not, he was a natural hot head, and continued to struggle with the pressures of life. There was a time when Rogers even threatened Truh with a gun. She, in turn, called her father, which she rarely did, unless there was really a problem. Truh's father said to her in anger: "I'll bring ***my gun!" Truh could envision how this could have turned out and immediately and frantically begged her father not to come. She did not want anyone to get hurt, but only called out of panic. They somehow got through this, another battle in the life of Rogers and Truh.

They were way over their heads in debt, and with the daily toils of making ends meet; not to mention, there was no budget or attempt to manage money. They got paid, bought booze, lived from week to week, while not counting the cost of what was ahead. The pressure mounted and mounted until Rogers began to take it out more and more on Truh. There would be more and more beatings, more and more often, and it would get so bad that the police would be called. But, as the police approached, Rogers would pour it on with crying and begging: "Please don't tell! I'm gonna do better." Until there finally came a day when Truh had heard enough of her mother begging her to do something or leave. She had finally gotten enough of being pushed around, enough of the pain of physical fights that left everything in the apartment broken up and holes in the walls from Rogers's angry temper. She finally made her move and left. This leaving was only temporary for at least 4 or 5 attempts as Rogers was very persuasive in getting Truh to come back into their co-dependent comfort zone. Finally, there was that last attempt when she really did not return to the situation. This was after Truh found herself jumping out of their car window in the dead of winter, running down the cold pavement with no shoes on her feet as Rogers threatened her to stay in the car while he was recklessly driving under the influence. Truh realized that Rogers was not and could not be responsible for his actions unless he got professional help. So she took responsibility and got out. This story could be dragged out with all of the details of the gore and blood but that is not what this book is about; it is about the fact that Truh got out alive and Rogers eventually made the necessary changes in his life to become a great man. But, not without a fight; they both went through some horrendous and brave encounters to get to the place that God had in mind for them. It is called walking in your destiny. Also, the book is about the fact that you have a chance to get out and make better of your life. It may sound so simple and easy, cut and dry, that Truh got out and all was well. No, that is absolutely not the exact way it happened; it is most nearly never that way in the struggles of a survivor of abuse. There was a missing link.

Abuser vs. Victim

Chapter 10:

The Missing Link

The missing link that so many people overlook is the fact that there are several compartments to our lives determining how we move through love, hate, living and dying. This missing link is huge and most importantly, it will set you up for either life or death. The missing link is your spirituality, your moral compass, your connection that affords you a relationship with your maker to whom you owe all the credit for survival, peace, happiness, joy, fulfillment, and prosperity in whatever you endeavor. Without this link, that makes all things work, you are destined for failure. The world over, people spend most of their lives running after things and money but overlooking the link that makes all of that stuff worth having. For every man, woman and child, there is an inner spirit, which entertains good or evil; there is a battle between the two raging on from birth until death. And unless we are aware of this part of our being, we will become blindsided as was the case with this dearest couple; Truh and Rogers. And for Truh to walk away from what she thought was simply a situation of domestic violence without a fight, would not be likely. Throughout this ongoing dilemma, there were dimensions of struggles for loyalty either for good or for evil. This is that spiritual side of man that I mentioned before that so many of us seem to overlook. Whether one believes in God or the existence of a Devil does not really matter as the battle between good and evil still plays out in the lives of every human being on earth. The enemy would not allow her or you or anyone for that matter, to jump ranks without a fight from him. He still believes that this is his world. Therefore he has set up traps involving drug addiction, domestic violence, murder, rape, family dysfunction and anything that undermines human nature, in order to keep us bound. Know that the enemy spends much time studying us. He takes the time to learn what we like and entertain, what we spend our money on, and the places we go. He knows so often before we even realize, what we are planning to do, before we do it, by the actions we have taken. He studies the facial expressions we make, the bodily gestures that we make sometimes even unconsciously. As with Truh, she had been repeatedly invited to get to know her Savior by a man passing out bible tracts everyday along the streets of the city near her job. Soon after her encounter with leaving Rogers, she was introduced to her REAL lover—- Jesus Christ by way of a simple booklet that was given to her from that man passing by while on her lunch break. Jesus took this opportunity to run after her while her heart was in a place that was not so distracted by her prior lock-down; while her heart was seeking help and redemption. This was a time when she would allow Him in, at a time of vulnerability and a time when she could hear Him and realize her need for something better. These encounters were threats to the enemy of her soul and he was about to lose her.

For the next several months, she spent time learning of Christ in a personal bible study with a couple of Christians sent her way. This, however, was a time when the enemy was enraged, and his plan to attempt to keep her in his ranks was amped up, and when she thought she was in a safe place, after having fled domestic war, was just the time the enemy put on his disguise and came in like a flood. Truh really should have gotten help by way of professional counseling and had someone to direct her into the way she should go. But she did what so many of us do: she just picked up her life after she had been battered and bruised and just went with the next step and carried on. This, for her, meant, to join a church, meet new friends, and forget the past. Not exactly. The enemy is one of the first persons to enter the church when the doors are open each week for worship. He knew of her great qualities, gifts, talents, and her heart for service that could be used for the kingdom of God. Therefore, he was determined to keep her in his ranks, so he did what any good Lieutenant would do. He fought for her, and he fought, and he fought. He was not giving up. But neither was Christ giving up on such a precious soul. Truh was leaving the worst physical battle of her life with great relief. Nevertheless, she was just entering the worse spiritual battle that she would ever fight and was not even aware that she had enlisted. You see, she was like thousands of others who don't believe that there is a real spiritual enemy! They have accepted the world's rendition of a fake, cartoon like enemy and what he looks like; a red mischievous, smiling faced figure with pointy ears and a pitchfork in his hands. They are not realizing he is truly a fallen angel (See Revelation 12-7-12), and his whole purpose in this life is to take their life. He will do it by any means possible, including the written purpose of this book. Misery loves company, and the bible speaks of the fact that he knows that he has but a short time.

Truh would be in this battle for quite some time before realizing what was actually going on. Being a babe in Christ, Truh had no idea that there is a great controversy over her life. She would not know of this battle or what this battle would look like and would think just being in the church and around Christians would be all there is to being a Christian. She will learn of her need to fight for her life and that this battle takes all she had, plus more. It would take putting on the whole armor of God each and every day and being aware of the enemy and his abilities so that she could fight intelligently.

Rogers, meanwhile, was pretty pitiful, as he lurked around with hopes to get back in Truh's graces and be reunited with her. But as he begins to realize that he had lost his grip on Truh, he then sunk further and further in his addiction until he found himself, living on the streets and eating out of trash cans. Rogers allowed his addiction to dictate his life to the point where Truh had to do what would break her heart; remove their little boy from his father until he would get professional help. He was only four years old at this time. Rogers did not know, but he was a part of the reason Truh did remain away and steadfastly determined to make it on her own. This move was a good thing, because they were totally codependent and no good for each other at this point. Poor little kid! He is in total love with both parents, but has to now be torn from one parent as they both cannot remain under the same roof without destroying one another.

Truh was getting to know more and more about her purpose in life as she studied her bible. She even tried to share with Rogers, but he was only allowing this as his attempts to get back with her. His desire to get back with Truh raged within him, but he never really settled himself into accepting Christ. She, after trying over and over again, decided it was not working and left Rogers to himself; not realizing she was also leaving him in the hands of the same Savior she was getting to know. Truh, after a year or more studying, gave her life to Christ and got baptized and began her new life in Christ.

Stay tuned for what happens to Truh, as the enemy tries everything to keep her in his ranks.

Are You Broken? You Can Be Restored!

BY: MORIAH NATASHA BERRY
TO: MOM (I love you!)

Chapter 11:
Life in a Whirlwind

On the surface, and for a short time, Truh enjoyed the life of a young Christian, but then found herself in relationships that would nearly take her life. Just as the list of characteristics for a domestic abuser includes isolation, manipulation, and control, so does that of the enemy. He engages you quickly with hopes to get you into his grasp BEFORE you get to know who he really is and make the smart decision, not to engage. Then, he will use his next tactic of "isolation" to move you far from your family, friends, and close associations as to have you all to himself. He brainwashes you into thinking he is enough and all you need and that he is and will continue to be your hero. Well, this is in fact, what was about to happen to Truh. She was so innocent and eager to live a good life, not realizing it would take more than having an interest. Her history of abandonment and codependency simply made her easy prey, just waiting to be lifted from her safe place and put into the pit of hell before she could even think straight.

About two years had passed and Truh now lived as a single parent near family. She had shared the truth of the gospel with her sister and they spent time with their new church family going for pizza, bowling, and studying one of her small study group's favorite bible topics: "The Second Coming of Christ". For the first time in a long time, she was feeling free from the burden of an addictive lifestyle. There was even a young man whom she had become close friends with or so she thought. He really appreciated the real Christian woman in her. One afternoon, after visiting with her, he totally surprised her by falling on one knee and pouring out his heart to her…" I know I don't have much, but what I have I'm willing to share it all with you. I love you with my whole heart. Truh will you marry me?" This was a genuine marriage proposal from the heart of a man in love with Christ. But unfortunately, Truh did not see in him, the qualities that she was used to and therefore did not accept his proposal. She felt that he was "too nice". What a sad commentary! Truh would have done very well to have entertained his proposal, or at least prayed about it. As it turns out he was quite the gentlemen with no history of abuse or any negative past and was interested in the Christ like attributes in her after spending time with her and seeing her grow spiritually. But as the question goes; "Why do good girls like bad boys?" Unfortunately, persons who are survivors of abuse may not see themselves worthy of good outcomes. Many, unconsciously, reject the good people that come into their lives. Their low self -worth causes them to believe that they could never be worthy of a higher caliber of persons. They are also unfamiliar with what they perceive to be a person of kindness. They are used to being treated in a threatening, less than appropriate manner and cannot see how they would fit in a world where there is no disregard for their feelings and the experience of being hit or emotionally challenged. Many a victim who is living a life of abuse has no idea that this phenomenon is occurring, and for years can live a sub-standard life, unless he or she receives some form of professional counseling. During counseling this phenomenon will be brought to their attention and many times they will be shocked that this act of rejecting the unfamiliar good things is happening to them. They will then require several sessions to begin to pay attention to the details of the effects of abuse and how to make psychological advances. During cognitive therapy they may address what "their belief" of what they have endured actually is. Working from there, they may begin to change how they think and feel about themselves. In turn, they will allow positive and good people and gifts to come into their lives. This is very important to note because the victim of abuse will continue in this cycle of passing up the good and being attracted to the bad for a life time, unless this cycle is broken. This is partly the answer to why people stay in abusive relationships.

Life in a Whirlwind

Truh really did not have a chance. Her only example of a mature and decent man was her father who she never really got the chance to know, coupled by the great fear she had of him. Then there was Rogers, the one she nearly sold her soul for. She loved him with all of her "codependent" heart but, he was not what a nice young lady needed. She was just blinded to what was good for her and did not get the counsel she desperately needed and made the choice based on a bad history. However, the story would have it that Truh set her eyes on another person instead. He was not, at all, good for her and ended up nearly taking her life, but she was saved by God's grace. This was just the exact example of the victim naturally being attracted to those who are just as "BROKEN" as they themselves. This gentleman expressed outwardly, many signs of distress and mental illness, but somehow, Truh, as a new Christian went all in. She even questioned why people at church could not trust God for healing him. Keep in mind that Truh at this point in her experience, was prom to choose what she was familiar with, and she trusted God like a child. She was so innocent and sympathetic to his illness and disposition, to the point that she went against all advice and nearly lost her life in the process. This particular story would take another book, but the following poem and commentary gives an idea of what she went through:

The Closet

The closet serves as a special place for me
A channel where death turned to life
Blindness, to eyes that could see.
The enemy wanted me so bad
He caused one nearest to turn mad
Mad enough to kill
To do a thing he would regret because,
for a moment
He could not feel
Feel the reality of the anger pent up inside
The consequences IF I died
For a while, felt like eternity: that precious
breath that God placed within,
Quickly diminished, like a balloon's
reaction to a pin
Fainting, fainting away, my whole life flashed
before me in one day
Thoughts of my family, friends, and my kid…
became sweet reminisce,
In my heart I hid
Thinking…"What a shame to die so very near"…
But my muffled scream…no one could hear
The begging and pleading for my life in my own
strength, did I try

*But this was not enough; I needed help
from on high
I know it was the Spirit who lived deep
inside of me
Who placed the words on my lips
"Lord Jesus... set me free!"
My mind cannot recall as I hung strangling
upon the wall
Just how I knew, on You to call.
No other words could I speak, for my breath was
almost gone
But you kept your promise: "I will never leave
you alone"
And spoke them, in my stead, for this was not in
your plan...
That I should be found dead.
The name of Jesus, I softly spoke, yet power
unreal to human kind...pulled the enemy
from behind
One would think a whole army came to my
defense, when through the air he went flying
As I ran away crying
The closet was supposed to be my end, but that's
where I met my best friend.
In my mind the memory will forever be sketched
The day the Spirit revealed His power and in the
closet, saved me that very hour.
Never doubt your connection with the Almighty,
He honors your faith and will set you free.*

As Chapter 11 continues: Consider the words of Truh as she shares her heart with you, the reader, who may be in a similar or worse space in your life.

For the girl, the young lady or well-defined women or man who finds yourself in a domestic and shameful situation; I write this for you. I am hopeful that you will come to know that until you find the strength and the know how to flee from that compromised place in your life; which you ultimately must do; you are not living your best life. I write as one having been there and was spared by the all mighty hand of God. Here is to the fact that there is certainly Power in the name of Jesus.

This was a day that came upon me in a time of folly, but yet it stems from me being in the wrong place with the wrong person. Sometimes we can get ourselves into situations outside of the protective care that our Heavenly Father has set up for us. Sometimes we know it, and sometimes we are unaware. We are always the ones who leave the side of God, because He keeps His promise to us and has said that He will "never leave us or forsake us" even if we are not living up to all that we know. His love is real. He is loyal!

One moment of folly at the wrong time led to a fit of anger which almost lead to the loss of my life, but God had another plan.

I was living across from my sister in a downstairs apartment in a metropolitan city in the south. A somewhat of a new Christian, I had been baptized in the last year. Fleeing from a domestic and violent lifestyle to a place where I thought was safe, only to flee into the arms of what was familiar to me, yet in disguise. I thought I had a new life and had left the old pain and suffering behind me. There were tales along the way, but as a new Christian, I did not want to believe that a person "in the church", "In Christ" could be what I was told he was. I asked myself, *"how could these Christians not have the faith that God could fix whatever was broken?" if, what they said was true?"* I was naive to the truth and all the signs I felt and saw. I kept my blinders on moving full steam ahead with the marriage and the honeymoon to boot. Until the enemy showed me the truth of the matter that people tried to convince me of from the beginning. It is said that there are times in a person's life when they cannot be told anything or discouraged from doing what they have planned to do. One of those times is in marriage, because they are no longer hearing with their ears, seeing with their eyes, or believing with reasoning; but are totally under the influence of their hearts and emotions. Such was the case with me. I was now living, moving, and breathing in my emotions and could not see, hear, or accept the truth. Instead, I refused to believe that something could be wrong with the man that I thought God had chosen for me. When, as it turned out, I had chosen for myself, and would not be convinced otherwise. I was still living a domestic violent victim's life and choosing the people that would harm me. God had sent every sign He could have sent. It was impossible to see them with my blinders on. I only really began to believe it when we were on our honeymoon and all of the glam and excitement had come to a halt. We were lying down by the fireplace snuggled in a beautiful mountain setting, far away from any help if I should need it. We were exchanging sweet nothings and embracing the memories of the good time we had at our wedding. When suddenly, I was hit by a ton of bricks! A thunderous feeling of extreme panic fell upon me. I sadly asked myself: *"What have I done?"* Not a good time to ask this question, right? I was alone with a man that I had been pre-warned might have the capacity to harm me. He was a man that had a record of extreme violence. Yet the man who I was determined to, and did marry, as I truly believed God could heal him even if he was broken. Well, I lived past that night and "The closet" is another story after several episodes of: "Are you sure you made the right decision?" had passed through my mind. In my folly of teasing him, a man who could not take jokes; I ran into the closet to hide as I laughed off his anger, or so I thought. But he was NOT kidding. He found me in that closet, which was in the back of our apartment. Again, completely obscured and on the other end of my sister's apartment where she could never know if I was in trouble. I looked into his red strained eyes and I knew then that the game was over. They were eyes that were raging, huge, bulging out of his head. He grabbed me by the throat and with what seemed like super strength, lifted me up with his bare hands off the floor by at least a foot. I tried with all my might to get him to stop and to understand that I was really not able to breathe; but it was too late. He was in that zone that people who knew him, tried to warn me about. There was no stopping him now. I saw my life flashing before me as in a panoramic view. All that I had ever done: my successes, the people I knew, good times with family and friends came up in succession. I thought to myself...*"I am only feet away from my sister, but she will not know. How can I call for help? What will be my end? My small child is asleep in the next room. Who will save him? What will happen to him after I am gone? Who can help me now?* I began to feel myself fainting away. It was like a fog. My vision was clouding and my thoughts were diminishing. I felt it was the approach of certain death. I was hopelessly accepting my fate of dying in the back of my apartment, in the quiet of my own closet, away from anyone who cared and could help me.

That is when the miracle happened! I was a praying and believing woman of God and He knew my heart and sent the help I needed in the nick of time. He came to my rescue and spoke the words out loud that my heart bled but my mouth could not speak. The force of the Holy Spirit and the Angels He sent came to my rescue like a bolt of lightning! They were unstoppable and unfathomable! Without having been there to experience it with my own eyes, it would have been nearly unbelievable. By the power and might displayed in that moment of my rescue, it is hard for me to truly believe that there could have been any less than a legion of Angels. But of course, it could have just been one, as they do excel in strength and power. Nevertheless, the Angel/(s) pushed him off me with such force that he was thrown backwards to the floor and I was set free. I did not linger to see what his outcome would be, but I fled as fast as I could to safety. When Jesus does anything, He does it well. My sister had been alerted by the Spirit of the Living God to go to her front door. She did not hear a knock or a stir, nor did she question her inspiration, but she obeyed without knowing any details. When she opened her front door, to her surprise, I ran inside and feel on the floor. She quickly, went over to get my son, who was still sleeping innocently in the room next to the offender as he attempted to take his own live, but was unsuccessful.

Again Jesus had been my savior. This was the third time. First, He saved me when He died on the cross for all mankind. Secondly,

Life in a Whirlwind

in redemption in my prayer of dedication as I accepted Him as a new born Christian and; now again, as my Knight in shining armor as He delivered me from certain death! Know that Jesus loves all of us, even the one who is responsible for hurting us. He died for us all and loves each one the same. His mercy and grace was extended, not only to me in that situation, but to my offender as he saved him from taking his own life and made sure he got help. God's church is a hospital for all who are sick and injured. We are all in need of a Savior and He shows himself a present help in time of need to all.

Are you that woman? Are you that man? The one who is in love but has on blinders? Are you suffering from low self-worth and choosing all that is bad for you? Well, be confident that if you love the Lord and commit yourself to Him, then He is certainly with you. But take the hint that we are loved in other ways than only the gift of romance. There is also that kind of love that is sent our way as warnings. We have those senses to alert us of the wrong paths that we could fall in. Just as with Eve in the garden, she was equipped with the same senses to alert her of wrong doings, but she ignored the sure instruction of the lord, and the world is not the same because of it. So we must now endure the hardship of living in this world of sin; the world that we were never designed to be a part of. We were designed to live in a lovely, pristine world of happiness for eternity. But now we, through Adam and Eve, are fallen creatures. Keep in mind that the fall engaged us in a battle for good or evil so we must keep our eyes on Jesus. He will be our only safe hiding place. Make wise decisions and follow the counsel of those who are close to you and have your best interest at heart. Seek professional help to assist you in unlocking the truths behind the choices you make.

For Truh, this relationship, of course, ended for the sake of her life and that of her child. But the enemy was not through with her yet. Stay tuned as Truh shares with us how this scary life-changing event affected her life.

Are You Broken? You Can Be Restored!

Chapter 12:

"Down, but Not Out"

"I was traumatized and in need of constant counseling for ongoing sessions until I would have a break- through and could began to grasp what I was dealing with. It was very difficult in the beginning to go through a single day when I did not see my counselor. I felt very unsafe without sitting in front of him and having him speak the words of life into my life to remind me that it was going to be ok. My life seemed to have come to a sudden halt and everything appeared to be moving in slow motion. All of this was just like a dream that I wished I could just wake up from. But, unfortunately it was real and I must deal with it for what it was worth. I must work through having the daily responsibilities as a mother, an employee and all of the usual daily tasks that life brings; while in the midst of trying to get a handle on the near death explosion that set my life on fire. It was found out that the person who nearly took my life did in fact have mental illness and it was a diagnosis with a prognosis that would take a lifetime of therapy to make any small improvement, unless God Himself should step in. The days were long and hard, we tried to remain a couple and pull things together, but without success. Whenever, I was in the same room with him, I felt that I must stand to my feet and never allow him to come from behind me. When we would sleep at night, I would only lie awake. His heart would beat so strong, that the whole bed would shake with each beat. There was a fear that I could not shack even as I prayed to the God that I totally believed could do anything. It got so bad for me that I could no longer live in the same apartment, so I began to sleep in my sister's apartment at night. This plan was short lived as he did not recognize my need for being in a safe place and simply did not agree with this arrangement.

I know that I am not the only person who has gone through hardship such as this one, where I almost lost my life and that is exactly why I wrote this book. There are so many emotions that one will experience while in a situation such as this one. It seems like I went through them all. I will try to share with you what you may expect should, this, or any other abusive encounter, ever happen to you. It is my hope that it does not, nevertheless, use my experience to be a warning for you. If you are in an abusive relationship may this be a preemptive resource."

What happens inside of you?

One may experience the crushing of your spirit, as a cold and fast wave against a sailboat in the midst of a sea storm. You are then left with a heaviness of heart that feels almost unbearable.

Your hopes and dreams all come tumbling down around you. That dreadful moment of utter embarrassment has become a reality. What will people think? The people who attended my fabulous wedding, my church members, and the people on my job who looked up to me because I was an up-standing citizen; what will they say? What do I say to them? How do I explain such failures in my life? What happened to my faith? Where can I run? Where can I hide? What of all the promises that my mate made to me? How could he? How could she just turn and walk away? Am I such a horrible person, or did I really know them? Who were they, really? How could my parents leave me so vulnerable and insecure? All of my friends at school are laughing at me! I feel so worthless and undone, unwanted and I can feel that the eyes of the world are upon me. Where can I turn now? I am so confused.

Once the shock and surprise of it all settles, the disbelief begins to subside, we began to blame ourselves for what has happened to us. "If I had only been nicer" or" if that last comment I made about him or her were left off." "Maybe, if I was a better daughter and kept my room cleaner, this would not have happened" "If only I had dressed up more and attended more functions at the church or the office" "If, only... If only... If only... Don't begin to play the blame game. Just seek the help you need to get your life back on track. All of the details will come out in the process as you get help.

Remember, there are human lives involved here, and for each human life there remain standard complications no matter how well things appear from the outside. We never can tell exactly what is happening inside. Only God and the persons involved know the intricacies of the difficulties for each.

Emotional disfigurement can scar a person but may not become evident for years and years. There can be subtle signs of damage such as a sense of shyness, lack of eye to eye contact, always putting oneself down, or even joking in a sarcastic manner. Then there could be more obvious tale-tale signs such as insecurities, feelings of inadequacies, failed relationships, uncontrolled anger, a sense of not belonging, not fitting in, hopelessness, and withdrawn behavior.

But if you aren't careful, these signs can be overlooked and can grow into larger problems leading to broken relationships and divorce, and the cycle repeating itself, which can require professional help. Even thoughts of suicide may come to the mind of the one who is hurting in silence. For me, there surely was a since of despair and certainly embarrassment. Since that encounter, my interest in mental health peaked and I have come to know that it is a real concern in our nation.

A word about mental illness from my view point: There must be, among our communities, healthcare facilities, churches, or within our societies, more places to reach out for help! Many people tend to cover all the bases when it comes to healthcare except when it comes to caring for those with "Mental Illness." Yes, Mental illness; such as in the case of "The Closet." Other examples, such as abandonment, which can scar in such a way that it leaves one with depression, failure to thrive, loss of hope; and all of these and other such conditions falls under the heading of mental health issues. We are so afraid to talk about mental disorders, problems, illnesses, breakdowns, or whatever name you want to call it, because we think this makes us look "crazy." We are afraid that people will look at us in the wrong light if we even speak on "mental illness." But, please realize that any time we deal with emotional pain or loss, it falls under the heading of mental, emotional, dysfunction and that is totally all right as long as we get the necessary help we need. We have physical illnesses, and just as our physical bodies get diseased, so do our minds and hearts. If we consider how closely they (the body and mind) are related, this will be better understood. One of the main reasons that I wrote this book is to be of some help to those who are suffering in that silence of fearing what people will say about them. Yet, needing a place to come for some relief and to meet with at least one other person who has been where they are and understands the pain, the shame, and the loss. There are those of you who spend time hiding, with hopes that no one will realize what is really happening to you, until you are out of that harmful and sad place. Then you will be able to say…"Oh, I was just having a bad day."

One of my favorite authors writes: "The relation that exists between the mind and the body is very intimate. When the one is affected, the other sympathizes. The condition of the mind affects the health to a far greater degree than many realize. Many of the diseases from which men suffer are the result of mental depression. Grief, anxiety, discontent, remorse, guilt, distrust, all tend to break down the life forces and to invite decay and death." Ministry of Healing EG White

What I take away from this statement is that there is no separating the two. If I am physically injured, whether it is a car accident or an injury falling down some stairs, or even if I am in a fight with another person; the effects of this physical injury will not stop at my body only. There is a relationship between the mind and the body that takes place. I must feel some way about what has happened to me (the body) and that is where the mental sympathy comes in; especially, if the physical injury is due to intentional harm. Say for example: a dog chases you and bites you on the leg. It will probably be something that you will remember for a long time. Not to mention if you are afraid of dogs or if you were young and helpless at the time of the injury. This mental anguish that you probably felt from not being able to get away from that dog may cause you to blame yourself, or even feel hopeless and incapable. This is where sympathy plays a part in the relationship between the mind and body. What about this example: In the case of spousal abuse where you are battered, when dinner is not ready when your mate comes home from work. This can happen either in male or female spousal abuse. This is an intentional event that perhaps occurs on a regular basis which would cause some stress in anticipation of that mate coming home each day. I can imagine the victim of this punishment racing to make sure that dinner is, in fact, ready as early as possible, especially if they don't even get home much sooner than their abuser. Well, can you imagine the sympathetic reaction he/she has to this scary situation? The mind is so adept at setting up a protective barrier when there is a need such as in cases of abuse, embarrassment, or any setting that would go under the title of self-preservation. I can even imagine the spouse who must have dinner ready on time or get beat; will find even in situations when her abuser is not there, that dinner time is a stressful occasion and she or he may even suffer from gastrointestinal problems because of it. These physical symptoms have no respect for place or time but can occur whenever the word "dinner" is mentioned, even in the absence of the demanding spouse. How sad this is for that victim, however, we look into the faces of millions of hurting people every day, not knowing that they are suffering. Statistic show that, according to the FBI, a woman is battered every 15 seconds, 2-4 million women are abused each year, "50% of homeless woman and children in this country are fleeing domestic violence, and"two in five of all victims of domestic violence are men.

 To ignore the fact that there is a problem such as mental illness which includes familiar conditions such as depression or other mood disorders, which we in the United States have done in so many ways is a shame, as we already have an epidemic on our hands. Not because we have simply ignored this problem, but also because of the financial breakdown- the hospitals, group homes are not available or affordable as they used to be. The struggle to maintain good help in the mental health facilities has become a huge problem. The mentally disabled are forced to find themselves in unwarranted situations of crime while just trying to survive. They are, in many cases, victims of domestic violence who are running for their lives. They are prematurely released from institutions due to the crowed situations and funding issues. They have no place to go, no support and accountability for taking their medications which will keep them mentally healthy. What is the outcome of this? We find them in jail as they have found it necessary to commit a crime to eat, and to get money for basic necessities of life. Sometimes they will knowingly commit crimes because they are afraid and need a warm place to stay the night, and with hopes to get a daily meal. Then, of course, they will be mandated to get back on their medications. There is a large percentage of individuals with mental illness taking up space in the jails and courtrooms and taxpayers pick up the tab.

Unchecked mental illness has taken a toll on our society. For example: The Las Vegas shooting- the man, who was responsible for this incident, from all points, appears to have been clear-headed with no record of mental health issues. However, something went terribly wrong somewhere in his thinking. Somewhere, he was probably hurt and did not follow up with help. Instead of getting help, he took all of his pent- up anger and displaced emotions on innocent people in society around him. He obviously needed a place to go for help and reprieve. We see occurrences all over the country and even in other parts of the world, where hurting people are hurting other people. This we see playing out in mass killings in public and private settings, (the movie theatre, universities, the white house lawn, college campuses, public schools…etc.) not to mention domestic abuse on top of this. The topic of mental illness is an important subject matter for any person who has found him or her -self emotionally, physically or psychologically injured, and, as was mentioned before, one cannot separate the effects that may have on the total person. In my particular situation of "The Closet" mental illness certainly played a part and propelled a world of pain and more suffering.

Now, that I have taken a moment to discuss a subject that is important but not talked about enough in the American culture, I will now get back to what happened next:

"Because I again found myself a single parent and had all of the cares of life to handle as the head of my home, I began to allow my appointments to get further and further apart. I eventually, over a period of several months, stopped going for therapy and thought I could handle things on my own. In other words, the immediate feelings of danger had passed. I got very busy with work and school. It was my purpose to put myself in an environment of higher learning that I could get the best education in order to provide for myself and my young son.

Time passed and I found myself dating people and continuing to look for love in all the wrong places. Without continued professional help, my need for restorative care began to be a vague impression. Jesus was still tugging at my heart, but in my mental state of independence, and not realizing I was losing my grip on Christ; I felt as though I must work this out for myself. Therefore, I did not surrender to Him totally; leaving myself dangling in front of the enemy. You must note that this was not a purposeful move at all. Like so many "nominal Christians", I felt that I was in a good space in my spiritual life.

I was still enjoying Christian fellowship at my church and living a life that I thought was pleasing to the Lord.

One day when spending time with my Christian friends, the conversation about camp meeting came up and I was invited to attend. This would be my first time at such a setting, so after hearing how much fun it would be, I decided to sign up to go. After going through that bad experience, I figured I was due for a good revival. "

In this next chapter, you will see how Truh, not only signed up for Camp Meeting, but for an unexpected wilderness experience.

Are You Broken? You Can Be Restored!

Chapter 13:
A Wilderness Experience

Truh went to Summer Camp Meeting with the church and it was an extremely hot summer in the South. There were the usual bugs, flies, and mosquitos. The air was stagnant and there was no escaping its smothering effects. She found it to be nearly unbearable as she perspired all day long and was awakened in the night drenched in sweat. She had an allergy to mosquitoes and would swell up double for each bite.

In spite of the brutal attacks from nature; the preaching, singing and fellowship were the best she had ever experienced. She felt a closeness with God that she longed to have all the time. Her time in God's presence while worshiping with all of the other saints would not be forgotten. Nevertheless, the temperature encouraged the aggravation of the insects and the bugs and heat got the best of her. "Well, this will never happen again!" she exclaimed. The enemy jumped for joy, because, it is his design to keep God's people from any soul stirring encounter like Camp Meetings. It was exactly what he wanted to hear. Truh's determination to never be a part of Camp meeting again would turn into missing out on this wonderful experience of heavenly bliss for the next, near thirty years. Unbelievable! Can you imagine missing out on work for that many years, how much it would have paid? How many benefits you would have lost by not being their? Well, it is worse having missed out on that many camp meetings over the years. She would miss out on the back to back preaching of the sermons that the preachers prepared especially for revival, especially for this time of year when people needed to hear a word from the Lord. Oh, and the singing from some of the best choirs in the world, prayer meetings early in the morning, midday and evening time. There was something for every part or your day to keep you on top of a pure spiritual high. Just what the Lord ordered for his saints, those for whom he planned to stay spiritually fueled until he comes again. This was like committing suicide, or worse, when inflicted by another; more like murder. The enemy went all out to try and kill Truh spiritually, to kill her very soul. He did not want her to live and when his attempts to kill her by way of domestic abuse did not work, he turned to another one of his best tactics- Meeting the people where they would least expect to find him- in church. But don't be fooled, remember that before he was expelled from Heaven, he was worshiping in the most melodious choir of the universe. Not only worshiping, but he was equipped with all one would need to be a choir director, (Ezekiel 28:13), so he knows exactly what he is doing when he meets us at church. Even there, he can distract us and keep us so busy with even doing the right things. So many people the world over spend huge amounts of time doing "Gods work" but how many are guilty of overdoing even a good thing and lose the real meaning of worship and the intention God has for worship. Some even end up worshiping themselves through the use of their talents and gifts and getting high on the praises received from others rather than honoring God and lifting up praises to Him, who is the only one worthy of praise. This is the enemy's plan indeed. To, one way or another, draw us away from God's perfect plans for our lives, while being fooled into thinking we are doing exactly what He has called us to do. But, this was the opposite for Truh. She actually walked away from worshiping amongst God's people as she once did, and lived a nominal Christian life. While still in church, (different churches over time), she was only there in form, but spiritually, she was not connected. The cares of this life keep her so bound that she could not even recognize that she had slipped away and had the form of Godliness while denying His power.

Well, fast forward nearly thirty years later, Truh kept her promise to never go to Camp Meeting again, but what she naively had not known is that over time, things got better on the camp grounds and the simple things she found herself complaining about

A Wilderness Experience

were changed. They put a new pavilion on the site, and the air conditioning was so cold now that people were complaining, not about the heat, but about how cold it was. People would now need to bring blankets and jackets to stay warm. The facilities were now gorgeous and large enough to house hundreds of people. The pavilion had several different rooms to accommodate whatever training was needed. So you see, the enemy's job was to fool Truh, just like he fools so many of us today. He has not changed.

You may ask the question, what in the world was Truh doing to have missed nearly thirty years of the great benefits of camp meeting? Did she move away or something? No, she did not move away, she was right where the story left her at our last chapter, but the only difference was that she had been given a special assignment. You may be asking…"What special assignment?" The assignment that the enemy has for each one of God's children, especially when we do and say things that gives him the hint that he can get a foot in edgewise. He is after all, trying with all of his might, especially at these closing hours of earth's history, to destroy as many of us as he possibly can. Misery loves company!

Now about this "special assignment: You see, the enemy wants to keep us busy doing everything we are big enough to do; to keep us blinded to the main reason we were created, to serve our Maker. He doesn't want to see us use any of our talents or skills, he especially does not want to see us help anyone come into the kingdom of God and go home with Him soon. He does not want us to enjoy life, fun, family, and friends. But instead, he wants us to suffer and die. One of my favorite authors whose writing is just as pertinent today as it was when she penned it many years ago, has an inside scoop in a meeting the enemy had with his followers. (the fallen angels). There he discussed his plans of what he would do in the lives of all he could. This was exactly what he did in Truh's life, and it goes like this: "As the people of God approach the perils of the last days, Satan holds earnest consultation with his angels as to the most successful plan of overthrowing their faith. He sees that the popular churches are already lulled to sleep by his deceptive power. By pleasing sophistry and lying wonders he can continue to hold them under his control. Therefore he directs his angels to lay their snares. Especially for those who are looking for the second advent of Christ, and endeavoring to keep all of the commandments of God."

Says the great deceiver: "We must watch those who are calling the attention of the people to the Sabbath of Jehovah; they will lead many to see the claims of the law of God, and the same light which reveals the true Sabbath, reveals also the ministration of Christ in the heavenly sanctuary, and shows that the last work for man's salvation is now going forward. Hold the minds of the people in darkness till that work is ended…"Go, make them possessors of lands and money drunk with the cares of this life. Present the world before them in its most attractive light that they may lay up their treasure here and fix their affections upon earthly things. We must do our utmost to prevent those who labor in God's cause from obtaining means to use against us. Keep the money in our own ranks. The more means they obtain, the more they will injure our kingdom by taking from us our subjects. Make them care more for money than for the up-building of Christ's kingdom and the spread of the truths we hate, and we need not fear their influence; for we know that every selfish, covetous person will fall under our power, and will finally be separated from God's people."

So, with, what seemed like a minor complaint, "It's too hot", "I won't be coming here again", the devil was able to get a foot in the door of Truh's life plans, and she never knew what hit her. This reading above about keeping the children of God busy and greedy speaks the truth. That is exactly what happens in our lives if we are not careful. With Truh, she was not only absent from the camp meeting and missing out on so many of the wonderful blessings that God had planned for her to grow and prosper in this message of salvation; but she would also be missing out on the family that came along with those blessings. The church family that she was introduced to at the onset of her introduction to Christ would be critical to her spiritual development and the enemy knew it quite well. What about the awesome experiences she already had with the people of God during her first few years as a babe in Christ? Nothing could replace them and the encounters of puppy love in Christ with her dear church family. These were special people who God placed in

A Wilderness Experience

her life to have helped her through a crisis, because there will always be a crisis as long as there is the Gospel. And what about the sweetness exchanged when she and her friends, her sisters and brothers in Christ would hang out at church all day, bringing their lunch and sitting around talking about the goodness of the Lord? These are special times that the Lord intends for each of us to have in order to keep us bonded and grounded in the faith. But the enemy takes our focus off these special gifts and places a complaint in our mouths and helps us to follow that complaint until he has time to take our lives, one way or another. Don't be fooled into thinking that while you are missing the fellowship with the saints at camp meeting that this will be the only thing that is happening. No. He always has a harsher agenda. For Truh, he planned for her to meet the worse times in her life. He wanted her to be on a battle field like none other and if at all possible, to lose her life and never come back to that group of precious people who are awaiting the coming of the Lord. While Truh had been duped into believing she was making the right choices, especially now that she had joined the family of God, the enemy led her into more abusive relationships and situations than you can imagine. She entertained more and more disloyal men who were only out to get one thing. She endured physical abuse, financial difficulty, struggling as a single parent, which is one of the hardest jobs in the world; along with disappointments, shame, fear and loss of hope. Truh was simply lost inside of herself. She could not understand how her life had turned into a complete whirlwind of events that nearly took her life. Her struggle went from nearly being choked to death, to fighting in public places, to being emotionally abused and led to think herself to be crazy. When, in fact it was the company she was keeping as had been ordered especially by the Devil himself. Because she had walked away from the family that could have been a help to her, in thinking she could do life on her own terms. This is the same lie he has told us since the beginning of time, ("Ye shall not surely die") but it only has a different look and feel, depending on how he brings it. He had her on this trip and was not letting up until he had her in his grips for keeps. The enemy became enraged as Truh gave her commitment to Christ and he then pulled blinders over her eyes for years. Around and around in the circle of abuse and confusion she went. It was as though there was a mark on her forehead to say to people, "hey, I like to be abused, come follow me."

Truh spent time with men who were not Christians as she too, fell into the lie that so many women believe…"There are no men in the church." So they go outside of the church and try to find love… here we go again… looking for love in all the wrong places. Of course, know that Truh was still looking for her dad in every man that she met; she would do that until she closes her eyes in death; that is just how it works. When things don't work out between a young girl and her father before either of them closes their eyes in death, the cycle will continue on repeating itself. One can prevent its evils by getting counseling, having mentors in one's life, and at least, educating one's self as to what is happening to them. But the craving for that man that God placed as a father in your life will always be there. One must just learn how to work through it and make the best choices in a mate. There is nothing wrong with looking for your father in a man, as a matter of fact, if your father has been a good example in your life; that would be just what the doctor ordered, to have someone to follow his footsteps and bring comfort and support as a father would.

Over those next infamous thirty years, Truh, however, would follow this maze of seduction by the enemy. But we must know that Truh was not fighting this battle alone. She had help all along the way. When she would allow for it, that is. Her Savior was fighting for her. He too, was relentless for her love, but he must have her permission and a surrendered heart. He is a gentleman and will not come in without being invited. Truh lived her life doing things her way, there was sometimes no invitation for her Savior, so Truh traveled hard territory and experience bumps along the way, "hard knocks" as they call it. When Truh was in tune with God, she would answer to His voice, but when she went on her own and did not follow His voice, she would find herself in very straight places.

There are many of you that are like Truh, going through trouble that seems to never end. Know that you too, are not alone. Let Jesus in. He stands at the door of your heart and knocks. His love can never separate Him from us.

A Wilderness Experience

Moriah N. Berry 10/10/2012

Justification
Romans 4:22-25
2 Corinthians 5:21
Romans 3:10
Romans 3:23
Romans 6:23
Isaiah 64:6
Psalm 51:5, 9, 10
Luke 18:13, 14
Romans 4:5
Ephesians 2:8, 9
1 Peter 2:24

- Psalm 32:1
- Romans 5:1
- Galatians 2

- Isaiah 53:5
- John 3:16
- 1 Peter 1:18, 19, 20

No Seperation From The Saviours Love

A checkered life, indeed, she lived. Sometimes in
the dumps of the
Lowest lows, and other times soaring high into
the sky. Many
Years would pass, events marking victories,
history being made,
Other times, stretching out her hands to God, and
asking "Why oh
God, Just let the hardship fade!"
Like a precious stone being carved and refined,
waiting for the day that she would shine. Her
life, she would realize is of God's careful design.
Loosing patches of memory of sad and heavy
days gone by…The plan was to keep her sane as
she pressed on and on, even though
She would without a doubt, cry and cry.
There is a saying…"Time will heal all wounds"…
Her adage: "Time will
Tell all and soon
Her cry would be…: Give back to me Dear Savior,
the innocence of a child, and help me to forgive
and forget the drudgery and pain often felt, mile
after mile

Close encounters with dope dealers, pusher, and the like, Fighting from corner to corner, what seemed like every night
Marking the places of her abode were broken pieces of furniture,
Holes in the walls, and every unimaginable plight.
Unlockable doors, returning used items to unsuspected stores.
Looking for treasures once had, only to find her partner's addiction got real bad
Her memory holds the scene of her child watching his mom,
Not only taking a licking but being drug from a car in the midst of constant domestic war.
Take away the memory of one bare foot and running.
Running with only the clothes on her back, running to avoid another cruel attack
Blot out the scene of violence remembered, bloody, blue and black
Even so, she's expected to have food on the table
There's no excuse, she's a woman, no matter the abuse!
Nearly fainting to her death, but saved by grace, who would know?
It was her mind's eye that looked unto her Savior's face
Jesus' name she called with bated breath.

Only by the spirit of God within! Never separated from His love, even in her sin.

Her thanks cry out to the Lord: "Thank you my Lord for your power and strength, as you demonstrated your love and sent your angel of light to save me.

From that last breath that went up... Thank you Dear Savior for accepting that cup, that cup that gives me life everlasting, that cup that gives me life here and now, oh and how!

The cup that frees me and says "my child stand up and be counted!

Though the enemy's hurls at you are ever mounted. "

The cup that gave me peace in the time of abandonment and helped me to pray.

To fall on my knees and say: Hallelujah!!

Thank you Dear God even for this very day!!!

Then the light came that shone ever so bright. In the crevices dispelling the darkest night. Revealing to her the undying love that only Jesus can give. A love that would allow her to live.

A walk downtown, nothing unusual, you see. But an Angel, dressed as a man, with a tract in his hand for me.

A hurry was par for the day. "Sister, God loves you" he said as he gave it away.

"Thank you she said, in a rush she fled.

But never did she think, by the Spirit of God was he led.

Back to her office with new found hope. What she thought was a note wrapped in a tiny envelope.

This was when I began to see that there could be no separation from the Savior's love and me.

Truh was NEVER alone, and neither are you. Stay tuned as Truh makes a great discovery concerning her true identity.

Are You Broken? You Can Be Restored!

Chapter 14:

I've Been Kidnapped!

It is the Summer of 2015. Truh was now the mother of two grown children and one grandson. She had indeed lived a checkered life. Having survived all sorts of abuse and what she considers the worst of them all- mental abuse. She stood in a place of hope and was determined to make the best of life. She'd made academic and career accomplishments and had done a bit of world travel. The amount of travel was extensive enough to let her know that the world she lives in is only a speck in the universe that her Father owns. Life had taken her through bends and twist to give her a determination to never let go the hands of her Savior. She had now begun to be more serious about her relationship with Jesus. Truh was gaining wisdom and growing in grace.

The table had turned, and the enemy had now begun to know who Truh was, and who she really belonged to. He took note because she had fought her way out and he realized that she was one of his toughest challenges and she was determined to keep her commitment to God. Truh had been enlightened as to why she had gone through all that she had to endure. She was now, very aware of her purpose, who her enemy was, and that she was on the winning team. She was excited for the call to tell others about where she had been and help them stand in this battle for life everlasting.

The enemy, of course, had not given up, but had slowed down his attacks; but neither has her Knight in shining armor given up; He who ever lives to save us.

After thirty years, the question again comes to Truh, from friends in her present, circle: "Do you want to go to camp meeting?"

"Camp meeting? I haven't been to camp meeting in I don't know how long?" Truh exclaims. Well, it has been close to thirty years, and oh how sad! She had been wrestling with the enemy for all of those years as she played on his playground. This was a dangerous place to play and so many go there with intents to play and leave, but they don't come out alive. Truh was one of the blessed ones who did make it out, not only alive, but with a restored heart. It is her plan and purpose to, not only be known as a survivor, but to bring as many souls along with her as she could. Now that she understands how the game is played, the enemy has a more difficult time alluring her to his playground and if he does get her attention, she usually immediately recognizes him for who he really is, and she steps off his turf and back onto safer ground. This lesson was not her own doing; but she had to learn through many hard knocks. She began to understand that she was not in the right place and began to place her loyalty in the one who gave His all for her and who would stop at nothing to save her from certain death. Now that Truh has been wooed into the loving arms of Jesus, and she has experienced what it was like on the other side; she is willing to give God another chance at blessing her in her life and at that point, at Camp Meeting. As my sister says, "life is a boomerang," whatever is sent out, will return again. Truh tried to prepare for camp meeting, but really was uncertain of what to expect. But she had a great friend who she met in recent years. He was her close friend and basketball coach. He personally invited her back to camp meeting to enjoy what he had never missed in the thirty years that she was accosted and held hostage by the enemy. He even loaned her a car to drive there and helped her with accomodations. She took the plunge and you will not believe what Truh's experience wrought!

Once Truh's feet hit the camp grounds, she saw so many faces that she had not seen in those lost thirty years. Yes, the people, the sisters, and brothers that she walked away from when she declared that she would never come to camp meeting again; not realizing with that declaration, the enemy would not only take her from camp meeting, but out of the assembly of God's people period. The very people she had bonded with. She was so pleasingly shocked! She immediately began to use the several gifts that God had blessed her with. When she went into the camp office to get her paper work she met people who remembered her for her massage techniques, and they raved about it, then she went up to the women's quarters and ran into another woman who had not been to camp meeting for a very long time either. While she was rehearsing how glad she was to be there, Truh could certainly appreciate her tears as the woman told her story. Then she ran into another person who asked if she would help interpret for the deaf, a gift by which the Lord had blessed her to first use among God's people when she went to a church sponsored health retreat. This happened over and over, until the end of the night. Truh had gotten a chance to use every single talent that God had given her. This brought tears to her eyes and she then realized that God was saying to her, "Welcome home, we missed you."

Truh was absolutely flabbergasted and she had an Epiphany. This was the same camp grounds; the place she swore not to go to again; yet the place that seemed like heaven on earth once she stepped onto its sacred grounds. The place where she met God again and began to see the whole panoramic view of what had been taking place in her life for the past thirty years.

"I've been kidnapped!" Truh Shouts aloud." I've been taken far away from home! The enemy has used my silly words of complaint and made them the worst words I have ever spoken and has used them against me and held me hostage! He has been trying to take my life while I was away from home!" she exclaimed. What a fool she must have felt like, to come to realize that she was on enemies territory all this time and thinking she was on God's turf. Wow! "What an awesome God! To stay with me and to bring me through all of those crazy relationships where the people did not give a darn about me. But were tactics of the devil used to keep me out of God's great loving plan for my life." Just like the quote said, "hold the minds of the people in darkness…" boy!, how Truh was in darkness, so tied up with work, school, and relationships and trying to make life work, but only without the full surrender to the only one who could make that happen- Jesus Christ the Righteous.

Now that Truh's eyes were opened, she was angry with the devil and vowed to never allow him the privilege to misuse and abuse her again. She was now more than ready to receive the love and protection that she was promised by her loving Savior all along. She was truly beginning to understand the Great Controversy that she was a part of and the importance of staying ever so close to Jesus. She set her heart on living a life with her eyes wide open and on purpose, while allowing Jesus to use her in any way to help those who will be blindsided just like she was. The astonishment she experienced when the blinders were pulled from her eyes gave her a true picture of how serious this battle between good and evil really is, and how there is no place to be but redeemed in the arms of Christ.

Chapter 15:

Redemption Draws Nigh

God's total theme throughout the bible is to redeem his lost people. No matter what book of the bible or what story you may read, it is about the plan that God has put in action to redeem or take back his lost children from the grips of the enemy. His great love for each of us is very clear. Truh found her family, which was not lost. She had simply walked away from them, by allowing herself to get tied up with the Devil. But she found that first love again and embraced it fully and brought back to the heart of God, her true heart. Through this incredible challenge, Truh, was able, even in her own struggles, to share this gospel message with her mother and family. The relationship that now existed and had existed for many years between Truh and her mother was a very loving and close one to say the least.

By God's amazing grace, and the work of the Holy Spirit, along with two hearts that were willing to submit over the years; there had never been any un-forgiveness expressed between them.

Truth, not only found in her a loving mother, but a friend.

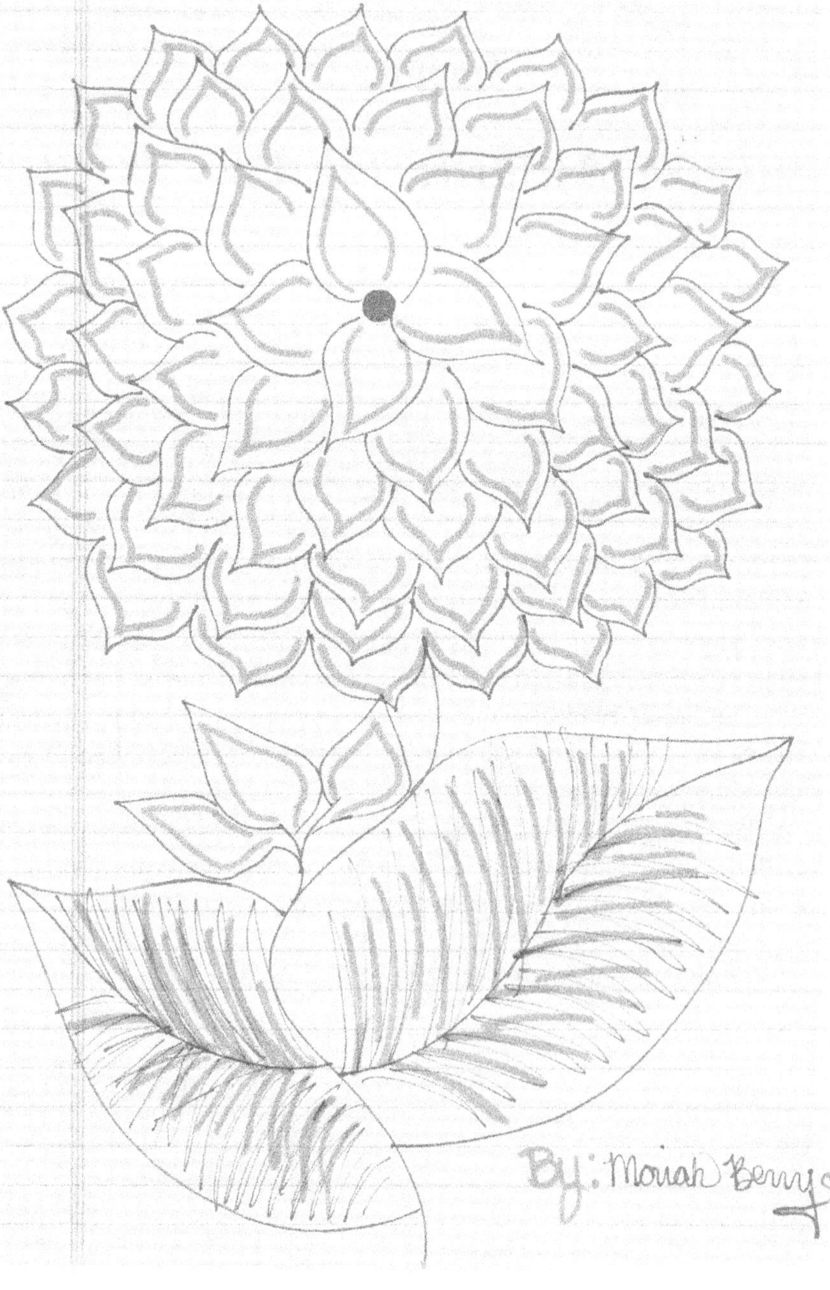
By: Moriah Berry

A Mother and a Friend

From the very start you were smart, above
all mothers,
A treasure from the heart
Raised practically without a mother to
call your own,
You had the tenacity to press forward
and run on.
The will and the strength to do ANYTHING.
You are a mother and a friend to me, another
like you will never, ever, be
You are loving, sensitive, and kind, sharing
yourself as though you were only mine
The cute outfits you made me, with your
bare hands, ribbon placed in my hair, not
rubber bands.
The homemaker, seamstress and cook like
no other, I
Was blessed to have you as my mother.
Truly dedicated, I could depend on you
to be there,
No matter when, no matter where.
You have been a mother and a friend for longer
than time can measure
I shout to the world, this has been my pleasure!
A visionary, exceptional and certainly not
the ordinary
Beautiful and awesome to look upon, as you've
put health and wellness in place, while you run
life's race.

Your silver crown shines all around, and
speaks volumes
Of your wisdom you see
Among the ladies, you are the towns envy.
Your trendy style along with your sincere smile,
sets you apart from the rest
You, mother, look your best
You have your own mind, and do things your
own creative way
With great spontaneity, you always save the day.
The social butterfly that you are, has helped me
in awkward situations look like a star.
You are the glue that holds the family together.
The glue that makes life worthy to share, the
meaning of the words,
"I CARE"
Throughout all my relationship blunders, my
mind often wonders; how you were the constant,
the Rock that anchored me.
You spoke words needed to set my weary
soul free.
A strong and courageous woman, way before
your time, you showed me how to draw the line.
The line between what is important and what
is not-the line that separates the winners from
the losers,
And the haves and the have- nots
Your spirit is loyal and true and over the years I
have trusted in you
A mother and a friend, kind, but yet fair,
speaking words of fact, never putting on an air.
I give you credit for wearing so many hats:
teacher, counselor, a listening ear

A friend who shares a hug in time of fear.
You, my mother have been a true way maker, a mover and a shaker
Always ready for positive change, personal growth exceeding your range.
Always with gift in hand, you taught me how to be generous to very man
What would my life have been like without a mother like you?
I seriously do not have a clue!
You've shaped my character making God glad, by using every tool you had.
Endearing and forgiving is why I love you so
You are so special, I can't come up with words to say
I'm realizing more of the depth of your love this very day
The tears are flowing and crowding my sight, as I persistently write
About a mother the world will never know again
Please Lord take control of my hand!
A mother and a friend through the light and well as darkest of my days
You have been there for me and I give God total Praise!!!!
A mother and a friend who have stuck with me through thick and thin, a mother and friend to the very end.

I Love You Mother

"Your Only Baby"

Are You Broken? You Can Be Restored!

Stay tuned. Chapter 16 reveals when the seashells of Truh's mind will began to open and unlock the details of her past. She finds out that she has been in a battle for her life for what seems like all of her life.

Chapter 16:
The Seashells Begin to Open Again

Over the years Truh began to take care of herself in a way that she could be that person to show appreciation for the love that Christ showed her in His death on the cross. Through professional and personal, counseling, much prayer and bible study; she has found that the Seashells of her mind were now opening again and allowing for the history of her life to be written, read and heard so that she and others would benefit.

Her children are grown and doing very well along with her wonderful grandson. She works in professional careers, Nursing and Real Estate helping others. She enjoys playing the violin, reading, cooking, and taking long walks.

It was uncovered during an assignment that Truh was given during counseling sessions where she was asked to write her autobiography that she discovered a whole section of her life was not accounted for. That patch of time was during the years of her family break up and rearrangement. Truh did not even recognize that some areas were missing until her counselor brought it to her attention. There were clumps of memory loss about things that occurred during the time of stress. Parts were remembered up to a point, then large holes were there in the place of what some other family members remembered. This was the time when she began to take note and put all efforts into rediscovering who she was and allowing God to help restore in her His desired outcome. As must be noted, trauma and stress to one person, may be a totally different experience for that of another person. We are especially designed by God, but not one of us is just alike or functions just the same. How glorious is that!

Remember we are "fearfully and wonderfully made" in the image of God and He knows what He is doing in designing a body that will fight till the end to save itself. All things work together for the good of them that love the Lord and are the called according to His purpose. Roman 8:28

Truh, through long and hard efforts in learning the truth of what happened over that long history of 30 years, when the enemy held her hostage; had come to know just when the enemy approached. She knew when he took captive her innocence; and she had seen the effects of not paying close spiritual attention to why she had been held hostage; and how that caused a breech in the relationship between her and God. She now understands, like no time before, the importance of her connection with her Savior. She knows now that the enemy is just like the bible describes him in Genesis 3:1: "Now the Serpent was more subtle (crafty) than any beast of the field which the Lord God had made." She has learned to put on the whole armor of God and stay ever so close to Him in order to make it to the end and walk on the sea of glass with the other saints of the Most-High. It is a good thing that Truh has an innate desire to be in ministry, any kind that serves the Lord, because she now lives to help others to avoid the huge pitfall that she fell into and to rejoice in doing whatever ministry the Lords has in store for her.

Chapter 17:
Finally, I've Been Redeemed!

The beautiful love story of God proposing to His bride is seen in Exodus 19:3-6 Then, Moses went up to God and the Lord called to him from the mountain and said, "This is what you are to say to the house of Jacob and what you are to tell the people of Israel: You yourselves have seen what I did to Egypt, and how I carried you on eagle's wings and brought you to myself. Now, if you obey me fully and keep my covenant, then out of all nations, you will be my treasured possession. Although the whole earth is mine, you will be for me a kingdom of priest and a holy nation. These are the words you are to speak to the Israelites."

What an awesome and wonderful love story this life of mine has been and it is culminating with God, my Relentless Lover, making that final proposal in covenant to have my hand in marriage and total commitment to Him, just like He did to the children of Israel. How many women long to be proposed to, especially after learning of the strong character traits their suitor has. Just like in the greatest love story novel that you have ever read, but better yet, our Knight in shining armor doesn't just come to propose. First, He must prove himself worthy of your hand in marriage. All of the manly characteristics are exposed here. The Lord first reminded the Israelites (His hopeful Bride) of what he did in showing himself strong and mighty. "You yourselves have seen what I did to Egypt", He said. If you haven't read the whole story, here is a quick synopsis:

The children of Israel were being freed from four hundred years of bondage in Egypt; which occurred by no fault of their own, but simply because they had grown and prospered in numbers so huge that the New Pharaoh, after the death of Joseph, became afraid they would overtake his territory and his people and they would become armies to enslave. Therefore, he caused his armies to enslave the Israelites and put burdens upon then as to make brick without straw.

The people cried out to the Lord for deliverance and He heard their cry and raised up Moses to be used to set them free. God showed his great strength and power as He caused Pharaoh to settle in his stubbornness so that, not only could the Lord show off His power to the heathens that enslaved His chosen people, but also, so that He, as God, could show off His power and glory before His bride to be. He performed many miracles in the way of several plagues along with the turning of Moses' rod into a snake. He turned the water into blood. He sent a plague of frogs for seven days, the plague of gnats, of flies, of dead animals when all livestock- cattle, sheep, and goats were all destroyed. He sent a plague of festering boils that the magician could not even stand in the presence of the Pharaoh for the extreme pain; a plague of hail that killed every other living thing; a plague of locust, of darkness, until Pharaoh was allowed to submit to Moses' request to "Let His People go so they could worship Him. But even then, there was one last renege on the part of Pharaoh. So God got His people ready because He knew this would be the culminating quest- He had the children of Israel to go throughout Egypt and ask for all of the silver and gold. As by now, the Egyptians were terrified of the God, for whom Israel served. They were more than willing to give up their gold and silver. The second show of our Knight in shining armor was after He readied His bride to be saved; as He would ride through on His colt at midnight to slay every first born in Egypt. The Israelites were covered as they obeyed to sacrifice a lamb and place the blood on the door post to be a symbol of the Lamb of God. They were passed over and thus the start of the historical celebration of the "Passover" as the death angel passed over them and they were saved. The next morning the whole of Egypt wailed for death and pain.

Finally, I've Been Redeemed!

Finally, as God's Bride was ready for the great "Exodus," with shoes on their feet; spoils in their bags, and unleavened bread prepared to cook later; the Lord with a large breath, blew on the sea and split the waters as he parted the Red Sea so "His Bride to be" could walk on "dry ground" to the other side. The waters stood up like walls of stone. Pharaoh's Egyptian army came after them with one last attempt to prevent their exit. Then the walls of water; at the command of the Lord through Moses, as he held up his staff, came crashing down. The Egyptian army all drowned in the Red Sea and God's power and might was like no other.

Can you see the correlation as with men today, they want to show their might and impress their woman, then secure their hearts before asking for their hand in matrimony. This idea is original with God, except, He is all mighty, and who in their right mind would say no!

He reminded them in verse 4 "how I carried you on eagle's wings and brought you to myself." Eagles have the largest wing span on record, as wide as 7-9 feet! What a picture of deliverance! Of redemption! And Restoration! He then pops the question: "Will you marry me?", but of course with some special stipulations to obey all He says to do.

With any sensible and awe-stricken woman who has just been swept off her feet by a handsome, loving, caring, chivalrous, and powerful man; the answer would be "yes."

Well, friend, this is exactly what I felt! I've been redeemed! I've been restored! My Relentless lover noticed I was in trouble and came to my rescue. He knew that I was on the wrong path so He sent an Angel to make sure nothing would happen to me that I could not handle until I came to my senses. He checked in with me personally to see if I was ready for total commitment, but when I wasn't, He waited patiently. But still hovered over me and protected my way and came again and again to knock on my heart's door. When I insisted on being drug in and out of abusive relationships because that was familiar to me; He let me choose. Still He was covering me with His angelic padding. He never stopped wooing me. My heart was so broken by the daily devastation of fighting in the streets, being subject to drug addiction and emotional attacks, yet still trying to do life my way. Even when He knew that me and my baby would be abandoned and left to fend for ourselves, He allowed it; but added extra padding and held my hand all the way through it. That is, when I would let Him. He sent me hope and some really great ways of escape but I did not recognize His attempts as expressions of love and only, thought: *"This couldn't be for me! I'm not good enough!"* So as I floundered around, He stayed right with me. For years and years, this went on until I was nearly killed and simply fell as low to rock bottom as I could get. Then the light of His presence came on and I decided to accept Him whole heartedly. I began to look back at all that had happened in this whirlwind of my life. *"Oh, how clearly I see it now. I am so precious and an expensive jewel in the sight of the Lord!"* The enemy threw that blanket over my eyes and led me into a dark life of abuse, affliction, and confusion to keep me from realizing my worth in Jesus; my Knight in shining armor. He tried so earnestly to destroy me because he knew I would do great things for the kingdom of God. Now here I am and I whole heartedly accept His proposal. Yes Jesus…I will marry you.

Thank God I've been redeemed!

Chapter 18:

Tell the world- My Appeal to You

I look back at what Jesus has done to "my Egyptian army."- How He caused plagues to fall and then to strip the enemy of all he had and even took lives, when necessary, for me to be rescued and redeemed.

Friend, we are in a spiritual battle that began a long time ago in heaven and is still raging here on earth, and the enemy will stop at nothing to take from you, your connection with Christ, no matter how he does it. Whether it is through a failed marriage, domestic abuse, poverty, or drug addiction- pick your choice, he's coming. However, there is hope, but only in Christ. He is the answer to all of your problems, just reach out to Him and be sincere and He will take it from there. He has the redeeming power to pull you from whatever pit of sin and shame you may find yourself in. The struggle is for life, but we are victorious in Christ. Go to back of the book (the bible) Revelation 19:11-16 and see the man on the white horse who comes to save His people as the "King of Kings and Lord of Lords" No more shame, no more pain, no more fear, no more crying.

Chapter 19:
The Color of Abuse

Tears falling down my cheeks
Feeling of insignificance, pain's obscurity
In a world of insecurity
Shameful acts of self-disrespect floods my mind
as I self-reflect
The color of Abuse
Awful, unwarranted misuse
Misuse of my time, damage to a creative and
intelligent mind
Today it may be RED - the crimson of
blood on my bed
What's the reason nothing is said!?
Facing the public-scarred, battered, and bruised
When will the victim disclose the accused?
Why do I stand for it? Why must I be used?
The color of abuse is rainbows, stripes, and
sometimes plaids, but the
End result is always sad.
Locked away in loneliness and madness

Left with broken promises that facilitates sadness
The GREEN of jealously and envy
Fills the air and chokes away life forces
As the colors of abuse constantly run
their courses.
The subtle disdain of jaundice filled eyes
A result of episodic cries
Cries out for help, for love and affection
Only to turn into the hazy GRAY of a fatal
attraction

Chapter 19A:
The Color of Abuse

Living the life of the victim of physical and emotional abuse lends itself to some pretty ridiculous experiences. Unfortunately the abused will not have the courage to speak up about the one who is responsible for their pain. The color of abuse speaks of the interwoven codependent behavior that is a result of the sickness entertained by one who is captured by abuse and begins to go through that rainbow of colors that will keep cycling until she or he is strong enough to jump off the carousel and get help. In the case of Rogers and Truh, well, it ended well, but only after a fight for survival on the part of both parties.

Truh, blossoms now to tell her story. Truh realizes that it was not all her fault, but that she was actually born into a battle and had to fight her way out. She is now in a much healthier place seeing the light at the end of the tunnel; which sparks a desire to do what she can to help others, like you, who are walking in her shoes. This is what she always says, "It is not about me: I have been saved to serve."

Truh met the man in "The Closet" at camp meeting 2015. A voice called out her name. She looked back and there he was. It had been more than 30 years since she laid eyes on him. With a renewed and restored heart, she returned his warm and sincere embrace, as he was super excited to see her again. There was no fear. There were no hard feelings. They spent some time catching up on what each had been doing, the children, etc. It is amazing what God can do in the hearts that surrender to His control. Everybody wins!

The Color of Abuse

As for Rogers: You will be amazed at how well his life turned out after getting professional help for his addictions and anger management. He had to try three times, then finally it stuck; but he is a beautiful human being. He is that special person that Truh knew was inside of him from the beginning. They both were co-dependent, were too young to understand it all, as he did not realize how deep he was in . Rogers is now twenty-five years clean at the writing of this book.

Rogers did find God, on his own terms and is now a true success story. He got his life together, by the graces of God, and now lives a healthy whole life. While he was making his way back into society, he rented a house in the same neighborhood where he was struggling. He opened the doors of this house for the people like him, who were hooked and could not find their way back. He opened this place so they could come and get food and get cleaned up until they could get the proper help that they needed. He had hope in them just like people had hope in him. He and Truh never got back together as a couple, but they remain very close friends, even to the point that she went to his wedding when he married a beautiful young lady that he met in the city of his recovery. She had a little boy who Rogers adopted and Rogers never stopped, even with all of the drama he endured, loving our first born. They are still the "two peas in a pod" that they have always been. He was an awesome father, no matter how low he went. He was there as much as possible, through it all, and like his father, even though he was an out of control alcoholic, had a love for each other so strong that it lasted through all the storms of this beast of alcoholism. They are all alive and well, and as close as ever.

Rogers went back to school and became a Registered Nurse and is doing great things in his field. He purchased a lovely suburban home and provides for his family now of six. He is an extremely responsible man, father, husband, and friend, and a great man in the community. Rogers's personal recovery story is one that Truh has encouraged him to write for all to read. Even though He and Truh went through so much together, there is a completely different side to his part of this story that has its own miracle influence to bless the hearts of a nation. We need to hear more positive outcomes of the lives of people like him. This could only have happened by the Grace and mighty power of God.

So, the color of abuse, we can find in so many areas of the lives of people. There is hope for the co-dependent, the angry, the alcoholic, the one who has been abused and the accused. What is your color of abuse?

Are you Broken? Are you trapped in a whirlwind of the plot that the enemy has tossed your way?- domestic violence, drug addiction, stuck in depression, or simply lost in doing this life your way? Well, it does not have to be for long. First, recognize that there is more to it than that, it's not only that you are having problems, or that of hereditary disposition; but there is a definite spiritual component. Then, take the mighty hand of Jesus by faith. He will pull you out of despair, and give you hope and life eternal! Just like He did for us.

Devotionals and Self Help

A Masterpiece

I am a masterpiece…
I am a masterpiece of creativity
There's no limit to my ability
I am a masterpiece
I bubble over with the desire to move the hearts of Men
I can't keep still…
My hands, my feet, I'm bursting out of my seat
A masterpiece, ready and willing to release
Nobody's like me in creativity; the voice, the motion
Not even the mental notion
I am a masterpiece
Give me a stage, or perhaps, an open page
A platform and a mic…let me perform, let me speak
With great alarm
I am a masterpiece…so versatile, priceless and well rounded
Like a plug…I'm well grounded.
I am a masterpiece!

Devotionals and Self Help

Genesis 1:27

"So God created man in his own image, in the image of God created He him, male and female created He them."

    This poem speaks for itself. We are all made in the image of our Creator, but in a very distinct and personal way. There is not, and never ever will be, another human being with the same anything like yours or like mine. We are given gifts and talents based on our make-up and based on what we will do with those gifts, we are physically designed specific to our oneness, and we have characteristics that allow us to stand as unique and individual as the next person. As for me, I have been given a multitude of gifts and talents that I enjoy so much and have questioned time and again why so many gifts? Why me? And why do I deserve to have them. It was not until I matured more and went through some ups and downs that I first began to tell myself that this is God's way of telling me he loves me and this is the reward that he gives in exchange for my suffering. I must say that I have since come to understand how God, the giver of all great and wonderful gifts, operates with respect to his children and meeting out to each their gifts. I feel special and blessed and want to maintain the ability to use these gifts every day of my life to help others. I have also been given the strength to endure some extremely tough times and I do believe that they were also gifts that have given me the opportunity to have empathy and sympathy for those who will walk in my painful shoes and will be benefitted by people like me who have been there and done that and still live to tell the story.
    I am reminded of the story in the bible of the talents in Matthew 25. Well the Master left his servants with 5 talents, 2 talents, and 1 talent. After his return, he checked to see what they had done with their talents. It's not like he did not already know the end from the beginning, because this Master, of course, represents God. Well, as he already knew, the servants with the 5 and the 2 talents increased their talents double fold, (with investments) but the servant with only one talent would not do anything with what he was given, but he did want to give him the chance to prove himself.

I personally cannot understand why one would not use his gift or talent. It just isn't how I think. I cannot imagine living my life without these wonderful gifts and surely cannot think of wasting any one gift that has been entrusted to me. God knows, and I am thankful for this great blessing. You too, have talents and or gifts that I hope you have used, and if not, plan to use. If you are one of those persons who declares: "I don't know what my talents are"... then I say to you, you have not been paying attention, and especially if you are in touch with your Maker, you have at least one gift. So get quiet and spend some time trying to figure it out. What is it that you enjoy doing and would do for free? What is it that you do that brings out the bright side of you and makes your day? What is it that others always seem to compliment you on? This is one of the ways that you can come to know your gifts; God uses people to affirm the masterpiece in you. You may hear something like: "Wow, you are so good at public speaking, whenever you speak, it seems like everyone gets quiet and gives you all of their attention." Or something like..." You are a natural at calming the babies, they react so naturally to your voice." "You are such a good cook, maybe you should hold a cooking class." These are all examples of how one may be affirmed in his or her gift/talents. Next, ask God to reveal to you the talents and or gifts he has given you. I Peter 4:10 says that each of you has received a gift, employ it for one another as good trustees of God's many-sided grace." Keep in mind too that some of the gifts that are yours, will not be discovered until later in life, when they are needed the most ,as by that time, you will have wisdom to impart along with them. It is important to know that your gift will always be a part of you and will draw you. The old adage: Do what you love and you will never work another day in your life. Being made in the image of God, naturally makes you a masterpiece, for He has creative abilities, He is kind and gentle, He has the ability to calm storms, He is a healer, and the list goes on. Now go and find out what ways God desires you to be used for others, you are His masterpiece.

Celebration

Never go where you are simply tolerated!
But, always where you are celebrated!
Swing the door wide open to a crowd
awaiting you...
Feel confident and warm through and through.
Knowing and believing they, are there because
their love for you is true.
With your biggest smile, light the room aglow
Letting the warmth of your insides show
Don't wait for a smile in response, know with
yours, it happened all at once.
Be free to be yourself
Relax,
Release
You're in CELEBRATION!!!
Be at peace!
Take down your guards, throw them far away...
Enjoy life, health, and this brand-new day!
Never mind your insecurities
They will never hinder here
For you are with real people
Who hold you very dear
Celebrate your life style, never feel you
are on trial!
This is not a case of self-denial.
Never go where you are simply tolerated, but
where you are CELEBRATED!!!

Are You Broken? You Can Be Restored!

Psalms 128:5

"Yes, they shall sing the praises of the Lord, and joyfully celebrate His mighty acts. For great is the Glory of the Lord."

Celebration is one of my favorite poems, because it speaks to the side of me that embraces the freedom of just being who I am. If you are anything like me, you have lived too many years allowing the world, or maybe your own particular surroundings, to dictate who you are or who you should be. They dictate by the culture, the societal customs, the rules, and regulations of the day. The comments people make, the way they dress and expect others around them to follow suit. We, for so long and really too long, have lived behind the terror of not fitting the mold, not fitting in, or not being accepted if I should just simply be who I am. I never really knew what to say, what to wear, when to act and how, etc, etc, etc. Well, one day I was listening to a sermon, by a preacher named Pastor Paula White. She was preaching about this same topic of being yourself when, she used the now, "indelible" phrase..." Never go where you are simply tolerated, but where you are celebrated". *"Well!!!"*, I thought to myself, that is exactly what I have felt inside, but did not come up with the cleaver way to express it. So I penned a poem to express how I feel about this saying. This poem is a freedom of expression to be just that person who God designed you to be, no matter what others think, say, or care, you are. Ever since, I have heard that saying, I have felt better about whom I am, and am proud to step outside of the box to be me. Now I say to you, adopt that same theme for yourself, be free to be you. From this day forward, it is yours for the taking.

The perfect thing about this poem is that it reminds you that the guards you put up when you are in the presence of those who do not accept you or want you in their circles, will never have to be used. Why?; because, you will have made the pro-active approach of never choosing that harmful, hurtful environment for yourself. Now you will be at peace knowing that the place you enter, is a place that holds out the scepter as was the case with king Ahasuerus who accepted the uninvited but welcomed entrance of his queen Esther in the bible story found in the chapter 8:4 of the book of Ester. Queen Ester was a Jewish Queen who had been chosen by a Persian King Ahasuerus to replace his former queen Vashti. Mind you, the king did not even realize he had married a Jew. The story of Ester involves some very religio- political ups and down, which led to Esther being encouraged to come to a place where her life was on the line. She went before the king to save, not only herself, but her Jewish people. Ester had come to the conclusion that she would present herself before the king unannounced whether she lived or died. The story is very rich and shows how God always takes care of His people, and it would be to your advantage to read the whole story. The royal law dictated that if anyone, even the queen, should approach the king without being announced, it would mean sudden and sure death. But by the favor of God, Queen Ester was favored of the King, and the end was in celebration instead. There is safety and confidence in knowing that if the King held out his scepter, you may have an audience with him without the fear of harm. The bible tells us in James 1:17 that "every good and perfect gift comes from above," it comes down from the Father." So, when you are celebrating anything good about you, you are actually celebrating the goodness of the Lord. Now, make the choice in your life today to choose who will be in control: the tolerated or celebrated?

Reflection:

1. Write down three insecurities that have caused you to feel unlikely to celebrate who you are.
   a. _____
   b. _____
   c. _____

2. What are ways you can begin to turn this around?

After glow: If you are willing to try these ways; later write down how it made you feel to try a different course of action.

Silver and Gold

My mind... I want to open to pad and pen, and tell about where,
By God's grace, I've been
I wish to wake the dead from their sorrowful slumber and sleep
And tell them a story that their hearts will keep
Unlock the chains, the shackles and the bondage of defeat
You have skill. Don't stand still. Jump to your feet!
Rise and determine to fly with the highest eagle in the sky
The sky is not the limit, but limitless bounds,
If you only trust and stand on Holy ground
All things sought after will not dissipate
But do not wait
Knowledge without Wisdom is not much
Leaning on a crutch
If you seek,
If you search
If you dig deep
You'll find a treasure of silver and gold
That only to you, God, will unfold.

"If thou seekest her as silver, and searchest for her as for hidden treasures; Then shalt thou understand the fear of the Lord, and find the knowledge of God"

Proverbs 2:4,5

We all probably know that the surface is never where the real treasures lie. One must give a lot more than just mere surface effort to get to the real deal. The gold diggers of California in the gold rush, are a prime example of how we must dig deep. Of course, there is always a little bit of "fools" gold floating on the top, but real gold has weight to it and it will fall to the bottom. So, there we are. Keep searching, keep digging, for the weightier matters in life require a concerted effort of determination and persistence to find what we need in creating the life that God desires for us to live and share. The bible tells us to get understanding, and that in getting understanding, we must also get Wisdom. Lacking wisdom is like mopping up a spill without turning off the faucet; it just does not work. Wisdom is certainly that thing we want and need in order to know what to do with the knowledge. God has given all of us experiences, and in some cases, it is not until we reach a certain point in life that much of these experiences make sense. That's why the bible calls the gray-haired person blessed. There is a gift that comes along with that "hoary head,", at least in most cases. We are told in Proverbs 14:3 that "the hoary head is a crown of beauty and glory if it is found in the way of righteousness." This poem is written with the excitement of writing about the experiences of my life, the things I've learned, the hard knocks that taught forever lessons, the gained strength, and the wisdom and courage that came out of just living. It seems that I have my best work in writing after a traumatic instance has occurred in my life or the life of someone to whom I am close. I tend to write about hardships and negative experiences. These experiences seemed to have been the periods of the recipient's life that needed what has been written during the course of those negative and hard times for me. In other words, it's not all about me, but whatever we go through; is also to help others. For example: the writings and out pouring of the soul comes so easily in response to one who has lost a loved one. Words carefully chosen and shared in times of need appear to be the gift that God uses to comfort others. So be encouraged and keep reading, there will be something that will get your attention and just the answer to your heart-felt prayer will be written there. God has seen me through a roller coaster of events that made me wonder if life would continue for me. He has saved me from imminent danger, as the enemy tried on so many occasions to take my life. In my survival, I found it to be the time to tell others like you, and to uplift your broken spirits. Life has a special way of using our pain to be our gain. When we are in the midst of the fire, we cry, "why me?!" But when the flames go out, we began to see why, and come to know our purpose for the sake of others. We are saved to serve. Keep on digging.

Reflection:

1. Why do you think God calls knowledge and wisdom, silver and gold?_____

2. How important is it for you to have Silver and Gold in your life?
_____
_____

The Test

Feeling shattered, Stripped naked, and Blue
The search and catch ended, when I didn't
Even have a clue
As though my clothes are transparent,
Embarrassed to the bone
Wishing time could erase my actions of
this day alone
Betrayed and abandoned, these I know so well,
Re-visitation of my soul, so frail
Stand up to the challenge my friend, never again
will you give in
Though the temptations assails you and seems so
very strong
Hold to the right and Reject the wrong
Hold your head up friend, you've been
there before
Pass this time and you won't go there anymore!

I Peter 4:12

"Beloved, think it not strange concerning the fiery trial which is to try you, as though some strange thing happened unto you." KJV

The NIV version says it this way: "Dear friends, do not be surprised at the fiery ordeal that has come on you to test you, as though something strange were happening to you."

We must keep in mind that we are in a battle, a great controversy for our souls is in full bloom and we, along with the help of Christ, fight every day for our lives to be saved in the end. Paul reminds the saints of his time that even though we have battles, and trials that we encounter; there is a reason and a reward. He follows by saying we should be glad to be partakers of suffering for Christ, for as Christ has received final and everlasting glory. So shout! We will be a part of that glory in the end.

This life is funny, just when you think you are in a safe place and it is quiet, the storm brews up again. Know that it is all a test, tests that tries us until we are pure and white as snow. When one test is over, be ready, because, a new test will come. Don't think it to be strange, says the bible; that is how it goes. Once you decided which team you were to be a player on, the battle began, so don't be confused and second guess what is happening in your life. To be a partaker of grander things and life everlasting, we must be willing to accept whatever suffering for Christ may be thrown our way. This is still in itself, a precious gift from God, because in James 1:5 we are told : "For you know that the testing of your faith produces perseverance." And of course, we must endure until the end, if we are to be saved.

Reflections:

1. What test are you experiencing?
2. Are you ready to push through?

You can be victorious in Christ today.

"The Philosophy of Life"

What does it mean to live this life?
Should it be carefree or full of strife?
What about our friends?
Are they lasting, or will they come to an end?
Today, life may mean joy.
Tomorrow, all could be lost,
Only showing itself as coy?
Uncertainty lurks behind every closed door.
Hopes for great plans can end up on the floor.
Do we accept life's ploy to demean? Or employ help on the scene?
What does it mean to live this life?
Inorganic matter, animal or the humane
Freedom of growth or held to ball and chain?
Life is what you make it, pompous, modest or barely existent
But, to its struggles, you must be resistant.

James 2:26

"For as the body without the spirit is dead, so faith without works is dead also."

Life presents its daily challenges, so much so -that if we don't persist to stay on top of things, we could become overwhelmed and soon lose our way. There is a persistent pull at our strength and our dedication to the cause for life, and for dreaming. For many, merely existing, is a daily struggle. To sit and wait for something to happen that will get you out of a bad situation, is only a waste of time; especially, when most of our troubles have been self -inflicted. You must fight! You must not give up!

In the book of Acts, chapter three (3), the story of the man who was an invalid from birth gives rise to the fact that there really is no excuse. This man was unable to walk, but that did not stop him from at least trying to get to a place where he hoped to get help. He was brought to the "Beautiful" the gate at the temple. The bible does not say, but I personally don't believe this man was brought there against his will. With that said, it is imagined that his will played a part in the effort to get to that place to seek for help. Many people would give arms or gifts to support him in his disabled condition, so he waited with hands out, as Peter and John passed by. Verse six tells what the disciples had to say about that…"Silver and Gold, have I none; but such as I have, give I thee, in the name of Jesus Christ of Nazareth, rise up and walk." This man did not doubt or ask questions. He did not rehearse his disability, but he put "work" along with his faith together, and he not only stood up, but the bible says in verse. eight that, "he went walking and leaping and praising God."

I can imagine that if he had not been willing to put his works along with his faith, he might still be sitting there. This is a symbol of how it really works in our lives today. Many are stuck in abusive relationships. They are going through that same horrible existence every day but feel hopeless and will not act on putting themselves in a place to receive the help they need. You may not be a victim of abuse, but still feel stuck in some form of life's entrapments, such

Devotionals and Self Help

as drug addiction, feeling locked in fear and laziness, lacking the skill or education you need, etc, etc. There are resources around you, but you must do something in order to take advantage of these services. These resources may change your life for better, but, they will not show up at your doorstep. Do the work that will be accompanied by your faith in God that things can and will get better in your life. Resist the struggle to sit it out, because Faith without works is dead.

Reflections:

1. What small step are you willing to take to put yourself in a place to get help?

2. Who can you trust to help you with this step?

3. List at least two people and two steps you would like to try, in order to get to a better place or in a place where someone can help you.

   a. _____
   b. _____

See the resource guide at the back of this book.

Never Give Up

Reach for the stars in all that you do
Never settle for less, strive for the very best
Stand your ground
You WILL be let down
Pull up, pull through, and lift yourself higher,
until the night passes
Today is here, tomorrow you may never see,
and may not
Remember what yesterday brought
But thanks to God for what He has wrought
Never give up!

Devotionals and Self Help

Matthew 24:13

"But he that shall endure unto the end, the same shall be saved."

To watch the news today is just like picking up the book of Matthew and reading the 24th chapter, which talks about all that is to happen before Jesus is to come back the second time. There is hardly a note of good mentioned, but more violence, shameful killings, and disregard for law and all that is good, including God.

One day, after a long day of ministry; Jesus was sitting on the Mount of Olives. He had just condemned the Pharisees and the Teachers of the law of Moses for saying one thing and doing another. He began to contemplate what He was destined to suffer. With heartfelt regret, He mourned how the people of Jerusalem killed the prophets and stoned the messengers and even after every attempt to save them, they would not. His disciples came to Him and asked in private about the end of the world. They wanted to know how it would happen and what signs to look for. Jesus shared with them our daily news feed: See verses 6-13

"You will hear of wars, and rumors of wars, but see to it that ye be not troubled: for all these things must come to pass, but the end is not yet. For nation shall rise against nation, and kingdom against kingdom: and there shall be famines, and pestilences, and earthquakes, in diverse places. All these are the beginning of sorrows. Then shall they deliver you up to be afflicted... many shall betray one another... many false prophets shall arise and deceive many... iniquity shall abound, love shall wax cold."

Now, did that sound like the news? Which would be easier, to open your bible, or to turn on the television? We are certainly in a scary time of earth's history, but be encouraged. Jesus counsels us to not give up but to endure until the end of all of this and we will be saved.

If you are going through some tough times, Trust the "Word" of God, who is Jesus and Never Give Up!

That's a Sure Thing

Life's a sunset slipping up on the end of the day…
so she stepped without notice, far, far away.
So far, it felt like, into obscurity,
when surely I knew it would be soon that she'd
Reappear assuredly
Handling the pressures of the days with just the
right amount of forbearance
One looks to God in thanksgiving and gratitude
Realizing, all good gifts are of great magnitude.
The time and the place will show itself
When she will again return to the space, she left.

I Corinthians 31:12

"For now we see through a glass, darkly; but then face to face: now I know in part; but then shall I know even as also I am known."

Only God knows what you've really been through, and only He knows the heart transplant taking place. You will be strengthened and the world will know the witness you bear as you help others go through. I know, even though I wasn't there in your personal experience, I still know that through it all, you've lost pieces of who you were. You've also loss the innocence and freedom to explore life and the beauty of wholeness and holiness. But God will give it back ten-fold, pressed down, shaken together, and running over. He will first help you to find that person lost in the shuffle.

Abandonment-Whether by virtue of the loss of a mate, an absent parent, a broken relationship on any level is not the problem that we imagine it to be. These hurtful experiences are instruments our Heavenly Father uses to draw us close to Him. Once he has shown us through His charm, the ugliness of sin, we will understand it better, and that is a sure thing.

Run to Him my sister!- my brother, and know he has all bases covered and will make you whole. You can look to Jesus for strength and help. Your only help, He is your only help!

Now, it is time to ask yourself, realizing you have job to do, and a role to play in helping other hurting souls…Where is the light at the end of the tunnel?

There must be darkness to appreciate a shadow. Total darkness for the stars to shine in their ultimate brightness;

Low times: to celebrate high times

Loneliness: to rejoice with friends

Poverty: to relish financial bliss

Rejection: to know love

A dead-end: to turn around

Hardship: to enjoy good times

Stagnation: to jump for joy

Hopelessness: to bring about a change

Abandonment: to appreciate the real lover of your soul.

My Angel

Hanging by a thread of hope
Like an addict in search for dope
The heart-felt prayer I sent up
I'll never regret....I'll never forget
A prayer in despair...Lord, are you out there?
"No disrespect, nor hint of disgrace, but I can no longer run this race"
With a heart of compassion, the God of His word, lovingly heard
An Angel clothed in humanity appeared unto me
Ready and willing to set me free
"You are not alone...His promises are true....He will never leave or forsake you"
God answered the sincerest longing of my soul, lifting me and giving me strength to reach my goal.
The Angel in the form of a man
Came without hesitation to my very destination
Pulling me from the sea of despair
Reminding me He is always right there.
The reader and interpreter of my heart
Gave me a new start
I was not too small to be seen
Not too timid to be heard
God searched me, and read every word
The rubbish is now clear
I have no fear
The Angle, my Angel is ever so near

Genesis 24:40

"And he said to me; The Lord whose presence I walk habitually will send His Angel with you and prosper your way and you will take a wife for my son and from my kindred and my father's house."

All through the bible, from Genesis to Revelation, Angels are spoken of. This text speaks of the time when Abraham in his old age spoke to the eldest servant of his house requesting that he go and find a wife for Isaac. This was his promise: that an Angel would accompany him on his journey and provide guidance. And such it was as the servant prayed; providence showed him what step to take next.

There are instances where we read about the Angels surrounding cites during battle, the Angels leading the way of the children of Israel in the wilderness, Angels ministered to Christ after He was tempted by the Devil, Angels explained the prophecies to Daniel, Angels spoke to Joseph and told him when to leave Bethlehem, the Angels who worship God day and night in Heaven and the list goes on and on.

Do you believe in Angels or that you have an Angel by your side? Well, the bible makes it very clear that we have Angels dispensed from Heaven to help us. The Angels are a precious gift from God to each one of us. They are given the duty of walking with us along this long and arduous life of ours, to keep us safe, and to notify us of dangers unseen to the human eye. I am sure you have had an experience where you realized you were in imminent danger but yet found yourself on safe grounds wondering how you got out of that situation. Well, it was more than likely your Angel who has been stationed by your side from birth until you die. Don't get tied up in the myth that Angels are not real. The bible also speaks of Evil Angels which are just as real and are on a totally different mission. These Angels are those who were deceived by Satan and were kicked out of Heaven with him. They are here on Earth to taunt us and cause us to be lost. Revelation 12:7-9 states: "And there was war in heaven: Michael and his angels fought against the dragon;

and the dragon fought and his angels and prevailed not; neither was their place found any more in heaven. And the great dragon was cast out, that old serpent, called the Devil, and Satan, which deceived the whole world; he was cast out into the earth, and his angels were case out with him."

The bible also speaks of the Angels having the sacred and awesome job of writing down every deed, good or bad, in the books of Heaven which will be used in the Judgment. Trust that your Angel has lead you through some rough times and places. You may be struggling with continued insults by this enemy who was cast out to the earth. But remember that you have an Angel who excels in strength whose job it is to protect, lead, and guide you. Be encouraged that you are never alone and that your Angel is with you every step of the way.

Reflection:

1. Name a time when you couldn't explain how you made it out of a bad situation unscathed?
2. Can you pinpoint how it could have happened?

Over flow: This might be a great time to be thankful.

Are You Broken? You Can Be Restored!

Short Poems

The Golden Key

Tonight I sit so alone
As the man with my heart is gone
Finally, to claim his own
Knowing it was coming
Not shying away, somewhat afraid
Still hastening the day
"For my good", I say
This time alone to ponder,
What of my fate now, I surely wonder
I must be brave and stand against the tide
I must be open to the Spirit, as my guide
A story to tell the world
Something I must say—
Tell them –There WILL be a brighter day!
I won't be afraid to step out of the box and see
what awaits me.
For the end of this drama
Holds the golden key.

"Inspiration"

Inspiration comes from within
Inspiration without hesitation
To sound the cry of emancipation
To every man and women
To every boy and girl
Words to inspire, heard throughout the world
Hearts that leap to the rhythm of the rhyme
Heads that speak to the necessity of the dime
Be inspired
Live to inspire
Inspiration comes from within.

"Apology Accepted"

Time and time again
We hurt one another...from the closest of friends
To the next of kin
Who will say "I'm sorry? Not to repeat
such an act
Who will began healing and get back on track?
You Better go first!
Or someday, if we're not careful... in regret, your
heart well immerse
Step up! Be the bigger man...say those words that
will forever stand...
I'M SORRY

Colossians 3:13

"Bear with each other and forgive one another, if any of you has a grievance against someone, forgive as the Lord forgave you."

Be the first to say that word: SORRY. Don't get trapped in the game of passing the blame, even if you are not at fault per se, but make the best of the time and start to love and live again. Don't allow yourself, your family, or your friends, to get lost in the, "it's not my fault," and "he hurt me first"… syndrome. Take full advantage of the gift you have in forgiveness to one another and let the notion of hope flow again. Let your heart be open to being vulnerable to the people who you know you love, and you know love you. Let this principle also spill over into the areas of non-family or acquaintances. Take down your barriers that you think are protecting you from learning to love and share, and allow other hearts, that may be broken down and in need of a friend, to come close to you and befriend you. Remember, as the saying goes, "Hurting people, hurt people". So many of us are in pain as a result of being hurt; that, we don't even know how to live without putting up a shield. We are fearful that we will be hurt again. That attitude takes precedence over the joy we could experience in simply loving and appreciating people in our lives and letting new people get to know us. To love, is to be vulnerable. I must admit, this is a lesson I am still wrestling with. I know the principle of it but putting it in practice is and has been difficult over the years because… as I said. "Hurting people, Hurt people," I am a work in progress. Let's work this together.., Take the plunge… be the first…Say the words…"I'm Sorry."

"Giving"

Take away the war in my soul
Help me to find control
Give me peace in this life
Let it so obliterate the strife
A life worth living
Is enhanced by giving
Open up your hand to another
The overflow received, will be un-believed!

"Dry Those Tear-Filled Eyes"

Dry those tear-filled eyes
They will blur and obscure blessings awaiting
you and yours
Closing open doors
Babies cry when their boundaries are met
Or even when their diapers are wet
The cry sounds the alarms for others to teach
Helping, their goals to be reached
Don't be too proud, to shout out loud!
The stool is not too low
The ladder is not too tall
All things are possible for us all.

"Timid Love"

To follow in another woman's footsteps....
I could not do
You choose me, not I you
The mind's eye rivets days of past
Whys such a love mate did not last?
Beyond the memories and photos, God only knows
The river of love runs so deep
The heart vicariously she keeps
The mystery of love will not unveil
Secrets stories, no one can tell
The days, the weeks, and months go by fast
New love springing up with hopes to last
A love like no other, never to dismiss
Yet a fire is kindled by a new kiss
The ebb and flow of timid apprehension
Safeguards loves throne, relieving the tension
The heart will go on
One beat at a time
Cherishing new friendship's
Rhythm and rhyme

Love

Love is all you need to soften the blow
Love is all you need to give you strength to go
Love will open the channel of
communication and
Give the heart a renovation
Love is all you need to make the
impossible seem real
Love is all you need to change the way you feel
Genuine, unconditional love is all you need to
make you heal
Love breaks down the barriers of pride when
life's ills contribute to a broken will
Love is all you need to bring out the real you
Love will hear the cry of the desperate,
lonely heart
Love will give you a new start

Short Stories

"Freedom In Bondage"

Freedom, freedom, I sincerely seek
Freedom will spring from my soul...
In bondage, I will not be weak!
In bondage today, but I will not stay
My spirit kicks and streams
To have realization of my dreams
I can be true to myself and bring out the beauty
of boundless strength.
Set me free oh God, you said you would.
I await your resource, which I know I should.
My heart one day will burst with creativity
Soaring as I take flight...with eagles wings
beyond the highest height.
Open the flood gates, oh Lord hear my cry!
Give me wings to fly!
Get off me enemy, get out of my way!
You are defeated, this very day!
Move out of my way as I soar high
To a bigger and boundless place in the sky
Freedom from bondage...you say there's no way?
You just wait and see
My words describe who and what I will be.
No more bondage for me!

"In the case of Rose"

On a summer evening, Rose is preparing to attend a social event with her husband. She is excited but, at the same time, a little bit nervous. You see, Rose doesn't quite know what to expect, as her husband is one way at home and another way when they are out. She stands in the mirror of their shared Jack and Jill vanity in the bedroom of their suburban home. She is meticulously styling her hair in a way that she thinks is her husband's favorite when he glances her way and does "that thing" that he does. With a grimace he makes her unsure of herself as he questions her: "Is that how you're wearing your hair?" This statement, as simple as it seems, brings about a moment of terror for Rose. Her heart immediately skips a beat, and then the beats to follow are pounding at 1000 beats a minute, her palms start to sweat, and she feels a queasiness in her stomach. The hope of a good night out just took a hike for Rose knows that the game has just begun. She realizes that he is about to play his usual mind game that will be sure to leave her in a place of uncertainty about everything except the fact that, no matter how hard she denies it; he is not nice and does not mean her well. He very recently told Rose when she was wearing that same hair style, "I like that hair style on you!" which is the reason she planned to wear her hair that way again. You see, Rose's husband is also her abuser, and he uses a large manipulative agenda to offset her mood and to inflict emotional upheaval. But the sad part about this story is that she has, for years, known the backdrop behind why he does this subtle mental teasing. She knows that he has his own issues of insecurity which is usually the case with all persons who find the need to bully others. However, she dare not alert him to the fact that she is aware of such. He puts on a face and fronts a powerful, strong, and secure man, when behind closed doors, he is a jealous and insecure terror. Rose has seen him in worse situations and chooses to live and let live, if at all possible. At this point, after he drops a bomb and walks away, Rose decides to change her hair style based on his simple, but complex, comment. She puts her hair up, then she swirls it to the left, then she pulls it back into a bun, but now that he has caused the hairs to stand up on her neck;

nothing seems to suit her. Why? Because she lives to please him; she is the co-star in a codependent relationship at its peak.

Rose was a woman with a long history of domestic abuse, (physical, emotional and psychological) before meeting her spouse of several years. It appears that she attracts the very thing that she fears. She admits to having the most difficulty and long-lasting effects from the emotional abuse she experiences as opposed to the physical. The bruises and the cuts would heal. The swelling would go down, and the crying would stop; at least for the time being. But the unwarranted mental assaults just seem to play tricks on her mind and would never seem to let her rest in being who she once knew herself to be; carefree and optimistic. When interviewed, Rose would comment that she was made to feel so inadequate and was often belittled by the negative and cruel comments from her abuser. So much so, that she began to believe the unwelcomed description of who he told her she was. She struggled with accepting herself for who she was after she had been convinced over and over again that she was "nobody". Living a quiet life of domestic abuse, Rose, lived a lie, never divulging any of this to her family and close friends, but suffering day to day with hopes that it would get better. The day of their social outing was in the seventh year of their marriage; I guess Rose had a lot of hope that things would turn around. In reality and according to statistics from the National Coalitions Against Domestic Violence, this is a normal occurrence in our society, where the victim is afraid to confront and get help or to leave a bad situation but hangs on until she or he gets hurt. The reality is that none of us has any real and meaningful identity outside of Christ. If we would only search Him out and spend time in His presence. Then we would come so close to knowing Him and therefore learning our worth as it is in His great sacrifice that He paid on Calvary. Rose, finally, after being so frustrated with herself for putting up with abuse over and over again and knowing where the night was heading, just simply snatched her hair back in a ponytail and left for the affair. He never once mentioned again how it looked. Sadly though he went through -out the night complimenting other women, in the presence of Rose, on how lovely their hair and dress looked. He would then, turn and look at Rose, with a self-satisfying smirk on his face. This was repeated during the night and Rose felt her absolute ugliest. She had given up all attempts to look her best. She unfortunately depended on him to encourage her self-confidence and approval. Prior to meeting her spouse, Rose was successful in her career in public service, she was a hands-on type of person, fun, and with lots of energy. She was considered a "Jack of all Trades, Master of None." A divorced, single parent of three children with great potential and looking forward to a good life when she met her husband, only to find out that after all of his promises to be her all and all, he was everything she was hoping to avoid. Rose stayed until she could no longer subject herself to the demeaning attacks on her character and person, but sadly with the long-lasting effects that would carry over into her future life. When making her decision to leave, she felt hopeless, and fearful, but her back was up against a wall and she needed relief. She wanted so much to make the right decision. Therefore, after giving it as much thought as possible, she allowed her mind to ponder all that had happened between them during that seven-year period. She reminisced about the days she spent hoping he would not come home, the time when he threw trash in her lap as they drove to the park on a beautiful sunny day; a non-provoked act of ugliness, which was followed by a fight. This seemed like it was just out of the blue, but she knew his ways were cold and calculated. This fight culminated with her being nearly strangled and lifted off the ground by his bare hands in the presence of one of her children. She rose to the occasion at that moment though and called the police, as her mind went back to where she had already come from. She was not taking another beating! She thought of the times when she would go to work and returned to find that all that she possessed was put in the basement and the house changed around to fit his liking alone; without even being asked what she might like. She remembered being left with strangers whom he had invited in as guests while he was out of town. How she would lie in her bed not knowing if that strange person would come into her bedroom during the night, or even harm her children. Her heart raced as she thought of these times, which were longed to be forgotten. Her mind's eye riveted to the experience when they looked for a new home and she was super excited and as she waited to find out when they would go and see the first home. But that excitement came to an abrupt end when she called from her out of town business trip to find out that she was not a consideration and that he had purchased the home in his name only and she had no say in it, not even to lay her eyes on it, until the contract was sealed. Lastly, she thought of the time when she did have to call the police after he physically abused her, only to allow him to go free in her fear of receiving retaliation.

    Well, Rose finally made the decision to walk away. To live her life for herself, and to be removed from the disgraceful, humiliating, and destructive lifestyle that she was living. She would step out on faith.. But, as the saying goes, "wherever you go, there you are." She had fears, insecurities, codependency, and was unsure of who she really was. Therefore, her flight to safety was a celebrated move, but not without the inevitable truth of facing the demons she ran from.

Run Away Eagle

Run away eagle, run away, fly
Go up, up to the sky
Run away eagle, don't look back
Don't slow your pace
Run my eagle, to a safe place
There's no mountain too high
There's no valley too low
Keep looking up eagle, let your spirit flow
Eternity and forever, is your limit now
Life has taught you that strategy,
You know how
Run away Eagle, Run away- Fly
Keep your chin up -Focus
Don't stop and don't you cry!
Run away Eagle, the time is now
Run, Run, Run away Eagle
Run away fly
Your time to run is nigh.

Fleeing Domestic Violence

For those in an abusive and scary situation, you may find it difficult to get out. The narrow options for survival may seem bleak, (according to theguardian.com, 75 % of victims are killed during and after their attempts to flee) but keep your eyes peeled and your intellect sharp for, if you trust God, He has promised to make a way. Have a plan and avoid becoming a statistic by contacting the National Domestic Violence Hotline at www.thehotline.org or calling 1-800-799-7233 or TTY- 10800-787-3224. According to the same source. "Domestic abuse is the most under-reported violent crime, with the average victim experiencing 35 assaults before calling the police. Many dismiss the first few incidents as on-offs, and when the abuse becomes consistent, victims might feel too ashamed to tell anyone, or see the abuse as a private matter. Many are trapped in abusive relationships out of the fear of the consequences of leaving. You're most at risk of being killed when you leave."

According to Care2.com: there are 10 main reasons why a person who is being abused will not leave the abuser:

1. Lack of social support
2. Limited financial resources
3. Minimal work experiences
4. Child custody and support
5. Pets
6. Fear of being alone
7. Family or community pressure
8. Guilt for "causing" the abuse
9. A seemingly healthy relationship (episodic abuse events)
10. Fear of provoking additional violence.

Tangela and Zeric were the talk of the community; they were seen as respectful citizens from nine to five; Monday through Friday. She worked as a Neonatal Nurse and could be seen heading for work dressed in a sparkling white nursing uniform. Her nails were clean, and every strand of hair was in place. He worked as a mechanical engineer and was very pleasant, quiet, and helpful in the neighborhood. But surprisingly, every week-end, without fail; the un-relentless abuse would ensue. It was hard to tell who started the fight. But by the time the cussing and yelling was heard, and the front door would fly open; it was no stopping them then. They would throw liquor bottles at each other and threaten to kill one another. A total transformation from the people seen during the work week had taken place. I guess this is what the bible means when it says that "Wine is a mocker, strong drink is raging, and whosoever is deceived thereby is not wise." Their situation was double fold, as they both were alcoholics, and severely co-dependent and each fought one another until they were blue and black and lost a lot of blood in the meantime. The fighting went on so long and hard, that it always resulted in them both being taken away in what was once called a "paddy wagon." For those of you who may never have heard that term, it was a police wagon. It was a station wagon-type vehicle with a long back, and double doors that were swung open at once. This vehicle had a capacity to hold several people. The police would actually throw them in the back like animals and the doors were slammed behind them, but the fighting never ceased. A totally disgraceful event that happened right in the presence of their young son. He found refuge in a family across the street. The woman of the children across the street somewhat adopted him and included him as though he was one of the family. For many looking on, the question was "Why doesn't she or he just leave?" but many of the situations are more complex that it appears, as the above list, notes.

One must know that in most domestic violent situations, the victim will only leave when he/she is ready, no matter how severe it seems to the onlooker. That person must come to a point in his or her experience where they have had enough and they are either in so much pain or they are simply willing to take the risk to get out. There are some, however, who do plan ahead and carefully, and stealthily, attempt and free themselves from this abusive lifestyle. They account for the 25% who, by God's grace, get out safely. Unfortunately, this was not the case for this couple, they fought and fought every year. They never got help for their alcoholism and continued to live as spectacles in their community until he died of a heart attack and she died of cancer; leaving their son scarred with the embarrassment and emotional trauma that such a lifestyle brings. All of the help that is available to us now, was not available back then, as this case was recorded in the 1960s. They simply did not know better, and every one, they, the son, the neighbors, all suffered as a result of the ignorance; but now there are so many opportunities for successfully managing to get out of that deadly situation.

This does not have to be your story. Sometimes the door will be open when you least expect it to. Don't miss your opportunity to flee bondage, and a life of abuse and "Run A-Way," never looking back, as the adrenaline rushes and your feet pound the pavement for freedom. Whether by special arrangement, secret service, or simply walking away, be smart, but take the chance at safety. Prepare yourself for flight. There will have to be a person in whom you place some trust in to help you make the move. Perhaps this person can be a family member, church member, friend, or special authorities with your best interest at heart. Make an "important papers" file with all the things you may need at your next level headed for safety and give it to that person of trust. Your birth certificate, driver's license, social security card for example. Papers for your children, some cash for the run. This may be your only chance so take flight and know that God has a better plan for your life. "Run-A-Way Eagle." Run.

Reflection:

1. Did this story touch a nerve in you?

2. Are you that person, are you the victim?

3. Will you consider calling the hot line number today?

"Calm in the Midst of a Storm"

Tears forming, teardrops falling
Can barely see my way
Want to save face. Thank God! it's a rainy day!
Driving up the road, around the corner,
here and there
Stopped on a lonely dark and desolate fare
The storm is raging, the billows rolling high
Gotta be an end to the pain that causes me to cry
Suddenly my midnight turns to day:
Deer, gently, and surprisingly pass my way
Scrawny legs, just a teetering, boney knees
wobbling to nearly fall
More exciting than a trip to the mall!
Frolicking in joyful innocent play
Loving life on their first day
Doe's eyes, a lovely feature
Beautiful, graceful, new born creatures
Brown curly coat to keep them warm
Their beauty of movement quiets my storm.
God has a sense of humor and can so quickly
turn your midnight into day!

Psalm 135:3

"Praise the Lord! For the Lord is good; sing praises to His name. For He is gracious and lovely! (AMPC) Amplified Bible Classic Edition

Pounded by the Brute

One day when I was being pounded by the brute that ruled my life, I left home and rode around just to get a few minutes of peace. When low and behold: God had placed two unlikely creatures right in front of my car, to share His love and kindness mixed with a little humor. This took my focus off my problems and brought me joy and calm amidst what I felt was a storm.

He graciously covered my face with the falling rain and took me just off the beaten path into a sacred museum of graceful, yet clumsy newborn deer.

I immediately stopped crying with the surprise of seeing dear in the city area.

This all happened in a neighborhood right outside of the city where I had spent most of my life and I have never seen this happen before. I spent many seasons traveling from the city to the wooded parks and rural areas so that I could see some form of nature. So, for me, this testifies that it was a splendid act of kindness designed just for me. It was a special moment in time. I was that important to my Heavenly Father that he called upon his friendly creatures to bring a wonderful display of helpless love right before my eyes. They played along just enough to enchant me and let me know that God was especially looking out for me. I was renewed, strengthened, and calmed in the midst of my storm. I was able to return home and face the music of whatever the brute had in store knowing that I was not alone.

Don't' be surprised if an unusual thing happens when you least expect it, but when you most need it. Just like when the Lord used the Donkey to save Balaam: Numbers 22:28 "Then the Lord opened the donkey's mouth, and it said to Balaam, "What have I done to you to make you beat me these three times?" Read the story for yourself, you'll be glad you did.

God is able to do anything! This world and all of the inhabitants belong to Him. At any given time or situation, He can use anyone and anything, including animals, flowers, events, that He chooses, to bring about whatever conclusion He desires for the sake of You. He is so clever and is known to pull stunts out of His hat of miracles to arrest you from a drowning situation and bring you back to a level mind with hope. He is that kind of God!

"Fearfully and Wonderfully Made"

As I sit and gaze the snow,
Flakes are falling from unknown heights
To the ground awaiting below
Apparent as to why, my praise go up to the God
of earth, and sky
All praise be to God in simple humility
He alone, could create such majesty
My eyes rivet from the written pages
of His word,
Reflections of grandeur nearly absurd!
The gentle snow flurries seen under the
streetlight,
Are quite dazzling as they fall
throughout the night
How wonderful God's design of focus and lens
Dual human cameras, with the ability to cleanse
No delay or manual adjustment needed, only
appreciation and careful
maintenance heeded
The depth of design, no one could know
My eyes to capture every flake of snow.

God Saved Her Sight

The story was told of a woman who went in to her eye doctor to have an eye exam as her vision was worsening. When she was examined, she was found to have damage to her retina (A layer at the back of the eyeball, which is responsible for vision formation in connection with the optic nerve and the light that passes that area). Her history was that of domestic violence from a former boyfriend years ago. She had experienced blunt trauma from his boot as he stepped purposefully onto her eye. Even though the trauma was several years prior, she still ran the risk of losing her sight in that eye if she had not followed up with her doctor. She was treated with eye drops to lower the elevated pressure which was causing her sight issues. Thankfully, this procedure saved the probability of blindness from something that happened in her past. To say that blindness was prevented sounds so simple, but researching the anatomy of the eye brings a much greater appreciation for what she could have lost.

According to the Eye Institute, Auckland, New Zealand; "Despite being only just over two centimeters in diameter, human eyes have over 2 million moving parts. They can distinguish over 500 shades of grey, and over 2.7 million colors." Other resources document there make up to include: six muscles in each eye, seven bones, one suspensory ligament of each eyeball that forms a sort of hammock stretch, three types of photo recapture cells are in the retina responsible for color vision, rod cells, for dim light, there are between 770,000 and 1.7 million nerve fibers."

Wow!.. And to add to this, the eyes come in different shades of beauty while being the most important complex organism in our bodies next to the brain.

I certainly understand why the Psalmist proclaimed to the Lord about His wonderful works. The eye is only a small portion of our human body and the fearfulness in which God has designed it is nearly unbelievable.

Sadly, though, "In the United States, over 1 million Americans experience eye injuries every year. Blunt eye injuries account for over 60% of these injuries, and over 10% of all eye traumas are due to assault." www.thehotline.org

Physical assault resulting in trauma to the eye can have both immediate and lasting effects. If trauma to the eye occurs, urgent medical attention should be sought to treat any immediate damage.

If this message speaks to you, please get help now; see your provider for an exam if you are experiencing any problems. If you are not experiencing any symptoms still get regular preventive care.

Psalms 139: 14

"I will praise you; for I am fearfully and wonderfully made: marvelous are your works; and that my soul knows right well."

The eyes are known as "The windows to the Soul"

God has great plans for your life and He wants to you to SEE it all!

"Tackle Your Fears"

Fear of the unknown fools even the best of us
Take on your fears, Give it a big gust
You'll never know your capabilities that
undergirds the Fear
Until you allow the thing you fear to come near
Test it and try it, It may be just for you
Even something you've longed to do
Should you not conquer this time around,
don't give up
Don't sit down
Tackle your fears, Tackle the unknown
Don't let this enemy pull you to the grown
with your face in a frown.

"Fearful Carmen"

Carmen is a middle aged single mother, living in a small city in North America. She lives with her daughter, an only child, who attends college nearby. Carmen suffers with anxiety and sees a Christian counselor regularly as well as follows her prescribed routine for oral medication. She is a very pleasant woman, but she is constantly in fear of one thing or another. She doesn't work and spends a lot of time doing really nothing, other than worrying about what negative things that might happen. Carmen is not an unusual case, in fact, the bible has predicted this would happen, especially in the later days as we are nearing the end of time when a lot of violence and disruption would be seen all over the world.

Carmen was surprised when her counselor shared this text with her. "Finally, believers, whatever is true, whatever is honorable *and* worthy of respect, whatever is right *and* confirmed by God's word, whatever is pure *and* wholesome, whatever is lovely *and* brings peace, whatever is admirable *and* of good repute; if there is any excellence, if there is anything worthy of praise, think *continually* on these things."

He invited her to take part in a community activity that involved helping the homeless in her neighborhood. After taking part in this endeavor for several weeks, Carmen began to feel so much better. She told her therapist that she wanted to continue as often as she could because she believed this was more therapeutic than even the medication she was on for anxiety.

The bible tells us of a thing called "True Religion" in the 58th chapter of Isaiah, "Give your food to the hungry and care for the homeless, then your light will shine in the darkness; your darkest hour will be like the noonday sun."

True religion heals when we take our eyes off of ourselves and serve others.

Are you experiencing anxiety, stress, and fear? Reach out to someone in need and turn your darkness into day.

Searching For Quiet

Life is filled with noise and the struggle to search for quiet....
From the time of birth
Until again we return to the blessed earth...
We struggle- we seek for time of quiet...a time of peace, a time of sweet release
In our daily journey, we run, we hide..
Looking for a quiet place on the other side
This life is so very busy, and "noise" is indeed its middle name, but as we wait for peace, hold on and stay in the game
A life once lived, but now lying upon a cooling bed. For now the noise is over and the quiet is upon his head.
For there is no noise in the grave below
It's solemn, it is quiet, a place of constant mellow
Fall asleep and know...there will be earth's molestation no more
Enjoy the peace and quiet of the dust...and when times comes await the crackling of the home going rush.
The only sound you need to hear is that of the sounds of the trumpet of Christ's return coming near.
Asleep my friend in the grave. You've escaped the misery this world gave.
The storm is over, the noise is all gone. Asleep in peace, have great release this, you have earned.
The noise will never again return.

Suicide Wins Again

Riley had a friend named Mr. Zee, who, from all points, appeared to be the most happy- go- lucky person she knew. It was always a fun time when they got together. Their time was filled with laughter, and jokes. They did a lot together, and the time seemed to fly by because of the fun they had. He was an older person, with lots of energy. He shared his knowledge in so many areas freely. He worked his garden daily and was sure to bring Riley some of his fresh produce. Mr. Zee was also a patient for the doctor's office where Riley worked and he would, at times ask her to help him, as he would get turned around with his directions. This was no problem, she would go to meet him at a spot that they mutually agreed upon, and direct him to the office. Later, she would call and check to make sure he got home safely after he left the office. It was simply a genuinely helpful friendship, where they both benefited and enjoyed spending time together. Their relationship grew rapidly over the three years that they knew each other. Whenever Riley knew that he would be coming by, she would look forward to an exciting time.

One day, Riley received a call from another friend. "Did you hear about Mr. Zee?" said the voice on the other end of the phone. "No. What about Mr. Zee," Riley replied. "He's dead, he shot and killed himself yesterday." Riley was speechless for a minute, as her world felt like it was turning upside down. "This is unbelievable!, we talked just the day before and he was fine!" Riley cried out, as she scrambled for reasons to arrest her heart. She recklessly did a mental search for ways to understand why he would do such a thing; especially without telling her he was having a problem. This was a very dark day in Riley's experience and she often revisits the feelings that she had when she heard that sad news. It has felt like such a disconnection and a space that will never really have answers to close that chapter. It is now eight years since Riley experienced the sad news of Mr. Zees death by suicide, but it is still a sore spot and a question without an answer. She must simply accept that he is gone so suddenly and will never be in her life again. She must be willing to celebrate the time they shared.

Mr. Zee was one of those who searched for quiet in all of the wrong places. He obviously was experiencing problems that he must have felt were overwhelming and that he did not have the answers to. As Riley grieved his death and visited with Mr. Zee's family, she found that there were at least five other family members who had also committed suicide as a way to escape their pain. This was horrifying to learn, and Riley began to feel sad that she was not allowed to be that person who could have helped him. "If he had only told me, I would have done all I could," she said. "I feel like such a failure as a friend" said Riley.

This occurrence is all too familiar in our world today, and people do blame themselves and spend time reminiscing and accessing if there were any tell-tale signs. It is likely that you too, know of someone who has committed suicide. Feeling inadequate, hopeless, and sheer shock that someone you actually knew, and perhaps just spoke to, did not think enough of you, or that you cared enough for them, to say something. Perhaps you may have been able to help haunts you and will be a question in your mind that will not have an answer.

The struggles of compounded trials, drugs and alcohol abuse, mental illness, have led some to search for quiet in all the wrong places. The enemy wishes for our souls to be lost at any cost.

God, on the other-hand, is a loving God who uses the very tactfulness of repetition to bring about the changes necessary in our character growth and development. He Helps us to become whole and well-balanced Christian soldiers to occupy His battlefield. He is wise and knows just what you need to strip away the rust of stubbornness, the awfulness of pride, the boldness of independence. He knows how to get you to begin to dislike, even hate the things of this world that encourages you to cling to selfish ambition, and to hold on to people. He knows how to encourage you to put your total trust in Him and Him alone.

Some of us suffer with depression and other mood disorders, that places us in conditions of deep despair and we long to do nothing but sleep and run away from our problems. We find rescue in medicating ourselves into a place of "quiet" where we are no longer responsive to the calls of life. We are so out of it and numb to what is important at that time, and that is just what we want, an escape from reality. We rely on the drugs that depress or sedate our senses to the real call of life; to be responsive to a God who has created us for Himself, and to be used by Him for the benefit of others. The bible tells us in Ecclesiastes 12:13 just why we are here and what is expected of us: "Let us hear the conclusion of the whole matter; Fear God and keep his commandments; for this is the whole duty of man." But we allow struggles of this life to get the best of us and we find ourselves spiraling out of control and seeking for "quiet" under a rock or under the influence of adverse chemicals when these things will never be the answer. The quiet we really are seeking, is the time to spend in the presence of the one who cares for you and has a master plan for your life. Quietly seek His face daily. Tell Him all about it and allow Him to bring you to the real "quiet" place where you will find true quiet and peace that will not rob you of what life He has given but will bring life and order and allow you to be a help and a benefit to others who walk in your shoes. God is not the author of all of the misfortunes in your life, but He has promised that all things will work for the good of those who love Him and therefore He will allow some of these negative events, to take place in your life, but He will work it out for your good. Take abandonment-for example: what feelings are you reminded of? Loneliness, fear, isolation, and separation. What greater combination than these to pull you closer to the one who saves you from these painful experiences.

He loves us enough to not allow us only good as we would not appreciate good if we never have bad times. If you should have enough of these trying times, soon and finally, you will not only long for Jesus to be a part of your life, but you will run to Him and ask Him to come in, to be the Lord of your life, the Ruler and lover of your soul. Be careful when you search for "quiet" Find it only in Christ, open your bible today. There is no quieter place than in the bosom of Jesus.

John 14:27

"Peace I leave with you; my peace I give unto you: not as the world giveth, give I unto you. Let not your heart be troubled, neither let it be afraid."

Reflection:

1. Are you searching for "quiet" in the wrong place? Don't do it! You are loved, and God has a better plan for you.

2. See the resource/help section in the back of this book now.

"Race Trac - The Kidnapping"

A trip out of town, baby in the back seat...Felt a queasiness that something wasn't cool. Would I be someone's fool?
Driver went in to pay for gas. Baby asked for chips.
Glimpsed the pay phone across the way; Hoping to save the day.
Tensions running high, stressed to the max.
Reasoning at an all-time low. Emotions ruling the flow.
Took a chance to escape, hoping to catch sister dear, who lives so near.
One who dated and played the field- it would be pure luck to catch her standing still.
Ring, Ring- heart beating a trillion times a minute, pounding my chest, I couldn't find rest.
No answer, tried and tried again, still lost in space, no time left at the Race.
Oh no! Now I've been spotted. The eyes are bulging, temper flaring when finally she answers...
Hello, hello, hello, "I'm at the Race Trac down the street! Please help before to death, I'm beat!

Short Stories

From my hand the phone and cord were snatched...thrown to the grown, dangling as I look down.
Babysitting innocently in the car, not knowing he would soon be a legendary star.
Waiting for his chips, all he knew, is that, something was starting to brew.
With anger deeply generated, he threw me, slung me, pulled and flung me all across that parking lot.
Looking like a public theatrical performance for the world to see. No place for fame and glee.
Cries went up for help from ANY stranger with a heart. "Just call the police:
911 would be a great start!"
Beating and bruising me up and down, dragging me and my new bag all over the grown.
"Help, somebody please help!" I shouted.
The crowd mortified, yet entertained, still not offering an ounce of rescue. More danger, yet to ensue.
Finally to the car I am dragged and pulled inside, head first. I am thrown...into the car which he owned
Kicking and screaming to the highest, not giving up...things happening so fast, seeing flashes as I look up...

Baby now to his surprise realizing his parents are in the streets doing what seems to be a past time, fighting to meet a deadline.
Around to the driver side he went, hoping to pull off without a scene. But I openly bust the door again rising to the occasion of freeing myself and the boy I love.
Only to be pushed and chugged inside, starting the rough and speedy ride.
Off at 100 miles plus, my heart in my hand- oh ghee, what's the rush?!
Baby in the back seat- people gazing at my defeat. What a world we live in- no one yet to arrive to offer some help, from a crazy man in disguise.
The ride on the highway, tears and pleadings filled the air.
I'm so darn mad; I don't know what to say. Hoping my Angel was helping me pray.
I've been kidnapped, how could this be? Who would think that this could happen to me?

Proverbs 9:7

"He who rebukes a scorner heaps upon himself abuse, and he who reproves a wicked man gets for himself bruises."

Why do people in a crowd of criminal intent, not offer help to the one who is obviously in trouble? Because it will be at the risk of himself. We live in a society where it is documented in scientific studies that the nature of man is such that he is, in fact, a follower and seeks directions from his surroundings in order to decide what action, in the presence of others, if any, he or she should take. Sadly, even in an instance of extreme violence. There are very few leaders, but many, many followers. This was demonstrated in the case of my story, as I was openly beaten by my abuser in a public gas station in the presence of my child. Exactly befitting to what those studies have shown. There were several people in this story and time and time again I cried out for help, but no one came to my rescue and neither did they call the police. I could see them gazing at me and taking the time to watch every minute of it, but no one there, as the bible text describes, was willing to "heap upon himself abuse." They all kept quiet while they watched with great intent; as though it was a movie. This shameful event unfortunately occurs too many times in our world today. The National Domestic Violence website states that domestic violence occurs every 15 seconds. This is a world-wide epidemic.

God was victorious in setting me free from my encounter, and with His help and a determination, I have since not allowed physical violence ever again and have lived to tell about it. I feel it is my duty and privilege to write about it because people like you may be experiencing this same type of horrible abuse or worse. It is time to contemplate your plan of action.

John 10:10 says: "The thief cometh not, but for to steal, and to kill, and to destroy; I am come that they (YOU) might have life and that they (YOU) might have it more abundantly."

Thought Questions:

1. Does this story sound familiar?

2. Will you consider a change?

3. Please turn to the resource page in the back of this book. Use the resources now.

Short Stories

A Tribute To My Father

My father passed away in 2005 and did not get the chance to read this book or either know of my restoration in Christ. I write in his honor.

Good Bye My Father

Good bye my dear Father. I know where you've gone.
To a resting place, where peace is your friend, and to be left alone
Good bye my Father
How suddenly you departed
But God Knows how to deal with the broken hearted
I look at my feet as I come to kneel and pray
They remind me of you, for these feet were created using your DNA
Good bye my Father
In your grave you will not think
But I won't forget the memories
Of you singing songs by Al Green
Or calling down the hall "Oh Jill…I love you, and all sorts of
Things
The blue jean maxi coats of the 70's, the fun trips to the damn
How you fished in that Florida deep water, yet got me home safely to go and spend my quarter
Good bye my Father
Thank you for the Time you spent with me,
Teaching me how to write checks and pay bills,

Thank you for sharing with me, these life skills.
Now time has stopped for you.
And for here, time will be no more
But the times we had I must place in my heart to adore.
I know you had great plans to accomplish more in this Life, but
It is time to lie down and be relieved of this strife.
I could tell by the stamped envelope in your car, that you didn't plan to leave so soon, but sleep has arrested you like a butterfly's cocoon.
The bible that lay upon the foot of your bed, with pages turned
To the place you last read, the mail on the kitchen table never opened.
Still sealed with the mailing label.
The car parked in the Driveway; stood still from that very day, Will never again
Go, with you as driver; either near or far away.
The faces of your children
Remarks the imprints of Claim,
The family portraits scorched in Flames,
Seem like a hall of Fame.
Good bye my Father
The days that are given are only but a few, to accomplish in this life all you must do.
Life is as a vapor. Here today, and gone tomorrow,
Leaving upon your head, pain and sorrow.

*The call that caused time to stand still for me,
was unexpected and seems never to flee.
For the Master has plans that are not
yours or mine.
His thoughts are not your thoughts,
His ways are Divine
Good bye my Father
The tears that flowed seemed to
Flush my very soul, they came like great lakes;
My vision and focus to Overtake.
Time stood still. No questions asked, no
permission given, only a feeling-surreal.
It was Good bye to my Father, A place I did not
know. A place I did not choose to go.
Arriving at home…Cars parked without a driver,
Scooter roaming the streets, reminded me that
time waits for no Man.
Life is a gift and its end is out of our Hands.
By the homeless, the destitute, the business man
Of the courts of justice, you were known.
But now time on this old earth for you is gone.
You will lay in your grave in the peace and quiet.
The cares of this world
will harass you no more, as you await heaven's
open door.
The silence of the grave will provide a resting
space, this earth, until now, never afforded…This
special place.*

Good bye my Father. I've put my hope in God's hands

For I Thessalonians 4:16-17 shares his great plans
For the Lord, Himself, shall descend from Heaven with a
Shout, with the voice of the Archangel, and the Trump of God: and the dead in Christ shall rise first; Then we which are alive and remain, shall be caught up together with them in the clouds to meet the Lord in the air: and so shall we ever be with the Lord.
Wherefore comfort one another with these words."
I Read John 5:28-29. The pleasure was indeed mine.
A resurrection for a home going or a resurrection for the lost. Father, I pray You talked with Jesus and counted the Cost.
I want to meet you there, Father.
The first resurrection, you see!
The time when the dead will raise forever to life and be free!
Good bye my Dear Father, Good
Bye for now. I must go and again
Put my hands to the plow.
GOOD BYE MY FATHER FOR NOW.

Exodus 20:12

"Honor your father and your mother, so that you may live long in the land the Lord your God is giving you."

July 19, 2005

"It is 3am and I sit atop the tub at my mother's home. Why I arose so early, I'm not so sure. But it has been difficult to sleep and to take full course meals for me. I feel like I'm in a space of disconnection. I can't seem to pull one thing together with another. This is a time that I wanted to continue in honoring my father in his death; in preparing an elegy just for him. These are the times when I usually can write of the loss of someone special and dear to me. However, this time it is different. It's my father and my soul is not yet set free to write of what this really means to me. I am thankful however, that just two weeks ago, I spent time with him attempting to assist him with getting his life records in order for such a time as this. He said he was not ready yet, so we put the paper work off for later; but later has come, all too soon. I am most grateful that the last words to him from me were: "I love You Dad." This seems awkward to write, for all of me and my siblings lives we have called him Robert, his first name. But I felt while in a different space in my life, it was time to honor him by addressing him as my father instead. I could not be happier with the Lord placing that on my conscience and the change being made just in the nick of time. Now he may reap the benefits of this honor due him. For it is not the deeds our parents do that makes them honor worthy, but the space they occupy.

My thoughts have never been so far from me when I sit down with pen and pad. Reality seems to be so hard to grasp, as this is a space of lonesomeness, illusion, and confusion as though I am floating in space. I looked at my toes as I knelt down to pray in my private place. These toes were created with the help of my father. I could never look at them and think of another.... and it happened: the writing came as a flood and is so self-explanatory. I think of my Father very often, even more now than when he was alive. It is so easy to take what you have for granted. As the saying goes: "A bird in the hand is worth more than two in the bush." Take stock in the bird that you now have in your hands and don't miss out on what they bring to your life while you are searching and seeking after what is "out there." Take time to spend with that bird that you have right here, right now.

This picture paints exactly what I felt during this time of loss.

A picture is worth a thousand words. I encourage you to take comfort in the privilege to honor your parents, no matter your age or station in life.

Elegy of a loving father who left me too soon.

Reflection:

1. Have you loss someone and wished you had shown more love or spent more time with them?

2. Did you find that you showed- out at the funeral? That's what usually happens.

3. Take the time to write out a simple (or not so simple) elegy to them to get if off your chest and get closure; then burn it and forgive yourself and do differently from now on.

Free Writes: Language of The Heart

*F*ree writes are amazing tools to let your heart sing with no restraints and great freedom of expression. I learned to do free writes when I was in college as I took a class in literature. A free write is something that happens when you just open up your heart, put the pen to the pad, and let it rip. The heart and mind are in control of what you will put down on paper. It tells the truth of what is going on inside of you. There are no distractions, no ideals for what you want to write, no plans for the outcome, just a frank, openness within yourself.

Whenever you do a Free Write, you must not think of anything you want to write about. You can't take breaks between sentences because if you do, you will begin to "think" and "plan" and therefore the idea of a Free Write will end. Free writes are designed to enhance your creativity and allow you to feel a very special freeing of your spirit and allow you to go places that you would normally be afraid to travel. But this is a safe place to explore and really began to understand more about who you are and what is inside that head of yours; without spending money on a couch. For me, I find it to be a sort of therapy.

What is your heart saying today? Try it, give it a go. You will be surprised at how much you have to say about something.

Hard Love

Time can bring about a change
When one lets the bond of
Reality settle for less
Less the love, less the compassion, less communication,
Less selfless acts of kindness
Shared between two minds
That once thought alike
Alike in the simplicity of love
Shown in the innocence of a fresh country breeze
Shadowed and filtered through heartbeats heavy
With the dew of connectivity by oneness
Love at first glance
Love set up as gelled to perfection
From the breath of one whose eyes lock into mine
The love that will overshadow the rhythm of pain
Dancing against the vibes of a cruel world without gain

Freedom

Freedom to be who you are
No boundaries, gates or places of non-escape
Freedom exudes the body, mind and spirit
Embracing the roots of hair, down to the nails
upon your toes
Take flight in the world of open space
and grandeur
The birds fly high and sing, sing, sing
Join in this song of freedom
Gliding higher and still higher
To embrace the truth of the Freedom Ring
The ring that sounds aloud within your
quiet heart
Break free of the noise of being trapped inside
And pull off to new heights with stride
Freedom, you. Freedom from within
Be free!

"Time"

The time has come to let the light of strength and
peace shine out
The stars are hidden
The world is ridden
Ridden with darkness and fear
Bring out the light of comfort to share
far and near
People are languishing and dying in silence
Un-forewarned, left alone in their pain
Tell them, they have so much to gain
Where is that voice that should cry out in
the might?
To help those in darkness come to the light
And get it right?
Uncover the beams and let them shine...
Shout it to the
world
The hope of safety
Tell them with hope, and joy of mind.

"Shackles"

The storm of the man keeps
Pressing down on me
But I still stand up with my
God given integrity
The Cedar Tree of Lebanon
Will stand until no more within me
Shines the sparks that forces me to be free
Free to be liberated of the
Shackles of control
Triggered by insecurity
I still stand because I am free!

"Fabulosity"

Aspire to Fabulosity
Don't sit under a bushel
And empty spaces of insecurity
Stand tall and never allow the enemy to
make you bawl
Yes cry and cry, but never due to pain
Cry out with laughter and joy
In the season of rain
Rain that comes down like a flood of happiness
Showers of blessing not restlessness
How can you deny the Fabulousness of
what God has
bestowed upon you?
There's no one like you this world through
and through
Look in the mirror with a new expectation
Grant yourself the honor of being a
fabulous creation!
(Written in 20 seconds)

"Be Brave"

Go to brave times up high on a hill
Smile when it seems like dawn is near
Open air praise and up liftings to God
Powerful storms put on hold
Cause He's the one
The one to break through for you and save
you from harm
Don't be afraid
Look to God in the storm
Open your mouth, yell out loud
Hoping within your all and all
To be made very proud
Don't settle for less in money, or merit
Put your best foot forward and press toward
The high calling
Give Him the glory!
(15 seconds)

I Will Rise

Sitting under a tall pine tree
Contemplating all the things that plaque me
Determined to climb up higher
Putting my thoughts and dreams before me,
I pledge to
aspire.
No matter how heavy the load
How rugged the terrain or pressure from mental strain
I will maintain
I WILL RISE
On the stepping stools of criticism, distain and rejection
I will rise to the mirror of reflection
Looking in to see, not what I am,
But what I can be.
On the ladder built one rung at a time
I will rise higher, leaving my cares all behind
Life is unpredictable. Short lived at best
I don't settle for the mundane like the rest
Putting my mind to it
I WILL RISE higher,
I believe I can do it.

"You Say"

You say, I am the abuser….
How can that be?
I've never noticed any signs within me
I don't hit, kick or bite
I don't scream, yell, or fight.
Buy, you say…I am the abuser
The signs of an abuser can be so subtle you see
For the way I hurt people lives deep within me
What you see is not really what is. The teasing, the joking
Is not all for fun, but perhaps it my way of controlling
While I have a little fun
Control is a form of abuse that feels a need for power
Don't be deceived thinking just because it is hidden laughter
The one you're hurting is not the victim
of a crime.
Abuse is a crime punishable by law
Check yourself to see if your actions are raw
Consider the other person's feelings when they say STOP
It is their right you know, to protect themselves so let them go.

*Abuse is anything that forces another to feel
misused, less than, trapped, in
In other words, abused
There is a method to the madness
You took abuse, now you feel the need to
retaliate, but look
Deep within and understand just why you hate.
Search your soul and seek for answers to
why you abuse
Could that be the answer?
Abusers come in all colors, shapes and sizes,
Abuse can lead to physical and emotional demise.
You Say I'm the Abuser.*

"A New Day"

At first I cried
Fell like I'd already died
But now my soul and spirit feels
redeemed and ready
To take on a new scene
Pictures of the past are fading
I'm ready to step into a new day
Don't want any delay
Feeling strong, delicious, and ready for anything
To come my way
The prayer for redemption was released
The tears have dried, the pounding in my
heart ceased
No resulting let down, great anticipation, no
hesitation
Only looking for what is real
No running to be concealed
The puffiness around my eyes
From mid-night cries- is gone
Happier and healthier, even being alone
No feeling like I'm losing my mind
With all the games played on my ego
I'm still able to just let it go
No questioning my beauty, my talents
or my worth

Accepting my gifts and skills
All my God given ability as
Special trust in reality
Looking in the mirror, I embrace
My lovely sensuous body with grace
The red-toned skin, smooth and soft to touch
Bone structure of a young thang
How could I ask for much?
Much more than what I see
How beautiful God has created me!
More than this, I do admire
Wavy, dark brown hair
A smile with dimples so discreet
Awaiting the next beau I'll meet
No more tears for me now
No time loss trying to please the unpleasable
No more restless days and nights, full of fright.
Insecurities have vanished away as I
Secure my place in a brand-new day!
Up at 4 a.m., excited and strong
Ready and worthy to get MY new day on
Holding nothing back from those who await me.
Ready to bounce back from my misery.
Open the door to my new world
Ready and willing to give it a whirl!
Not afraid of commitment
Not afraid to love again
For loving always means taking a chance
A chance at heart ache and defeat

*Never giving up, looking forward to the
track meet
Bring it on! I can handle it!
Stepping out in faith
Head back, chin up, one step in front of the other
Feeling so much better, clear headed and strong
Proud of how far I've come along.*

"Hurricane In My Heart"

There is a quiet storm within my heart
Don't know how to brace it at its start
Emotions running high, don't wanna perish,
But live to be cherished
Unable to open up and release the pain
Feels like giving up everything
But where is my gain?
The dreamer in me holds on to the
promise of hope
Dangling sometimes on a thin rope
Flashes of lightening rips deep within my soul
The thunder bolts of heaviness overtakes
my thoughts
A way out is aggressively sought
The trenches of my eyes
Fill with the rain of pain
Overflowing and collecting against the brim
Chances of survival appearing slim
Please hush the noise within my head
Rescue me from these awful spells
Upon my bed
Rush in and save me!
Over turn this battle of nature and release the
fury of this
hurricane
I surrender my struggle as all my strength
is regained

2ⁿᵈ Corinthians 3:17

The Lord and the Spirit are one and the same, and the Lord's Spirit sets us free.

Many people seek to be free from their circumstances in life. Whether it is a job they absolutely hate, a marriage that is suffocating; or even an oppressive habit they may have that keeps them going through the motions of attempting to get free.

Well, if you are anything like most of us, we all struggle with some form of bondage, but the one thing we do have in common is that we wrestle with whatever that thing is over and over, year in, and year out. The reason being, is that, we are simply powerless to free ourselves from the bondage that keeps us in what appears to be hopeless situations. That is, hopeless without a divine intervention from Christ, as He is the only answer.

In the bible (2 Corinthians 12: 7-9) Paul often speaks of a situation of being bound by what he calls a "thorn in his flesh," for which he asked the Lord to relieve him of three times. It is still unclear as to what Paul is exactly referring to. Perhaps a physical ailment, a habit or an addiction of some sort; but we can see that it is for Paul a sort of bondage. He felt that it was keeping him from performing his best for Christ and even reasoned that it was allowed to keep him from being high minded.

Paul was given an answer to his thrice driven question for relief. The answer was not what he wanted but Paul accepted the answer and made lemonade out of what he could have thought to be a lemon. The answer can be found in 2 Corinthians 12:9 and Paul states: "And He said to me. My grace is sufficient for you."

This answer is a very clever and comprehensive answer from Christ. I am always intrigued at the answers Jesus comes up with, in answer to our myriad of questions. He always come from a different angle than we could even imagine. Yet the answers always work for any situation and that person is always blessed.

This same answer is what I offer you today, friend. God's grace is still sufficient for you too. Whatever type of bondage you feel you are in, it is a matter of looking to Christ and allowing Him to work things out. If He feels that that particular situation in your life should continue, then He has it covered. Of course, we know He will never leave you in a scary and harmful situation of physical abuse. We know the answer to that. Get out. Now! But for those situations that feel like bondage because you are locked into a mental or emotional place that you don't prefer, just change the channel and look to Christ. He has promised, He has your good in mind that His grace is sufficient for you.

With Christ, You may have freedom IN bondage.

"Feet Are For Walking"

Get your feet off me, so I can be free!
Feet are for walking and standing up straight.
Your feet on me is something I hate!
You say I'll never make it
Just like a rattle snake
You say just give up, you don't have
what it takes
I'm holding on to what I feel inside
Holding on to my unsung pride
A change is coming, coming soon
I will be happy and uplifted from
The doom and the gloom.
I'm gonna make it big, you'll see
God has placed His success in me.

Psalms 37:1

Fret not yourself because of evildoers, neither be thou envious against the workers of iniquity. For they shall soon be cut down like the grass, and wither as the green herb.

Unfortunately, we have all had a person who wants to boss us around and stop all prospects of success in our lives. Why would anyone want to do this? The devil is the one who is responsible for all the evil upon the earth. Well, we must be of the mind that they are under his influence. The bible sums it all up in John 10:10. "The thief cometh not, but to steal, and to kill, and to destroy." We are cautioned to not spend any amount of time worrying about that.

There is such a thing as spiritual warfare where we are not really contending with people for whom you actually see, even though it appears that they are the culprit for all of the inappropriate behavior and unwarranted discourses. If they are not grounded in Christ, they are subject to anything. So when people try and step on you and treat you like nothing, don't hold it against them per se, remember that the Devil is very anxious as his time is running out quickly and he is tempting as many people as he can to be lost with him. You know that misery loves company, and that is proven in Revelation 12:12 where is says: "Woe to the earth and the seas because the devil has come down to you, having great wrath knowing that he has only a short time."

Be of good courage, because the Lord has promised that He will take care of it, whatever it is, as vengeance is the Lords.

Take to heart the rest of the text in John 10:10. "I am come that they might have life, and that they might have it more abundantly."

"Never Alone"

Never alone?
How could this be?
It seems, no one is walking with me!
In the midst of a crowd or with my church members dear,
I feel lonely, even a bit of fear.
They say I am never alone
Jesus is with, even me
But sometimes, I feel to disagree
Don't depend on your feelings
To do so, is a crime!
They will let you down, every time
To be with you always
God's promises are made
Written on pages, never to fade

Hebrews 13:5

"Never will I leave you, nor forsake you"

There was a story of conjoined (Siamese) twins, young ladies in their early twenties. One of the twins developed a heart condition and the circulation of both the young ladies was at risk from further complications. This condition required them to undergo an operation to separate from one another. This was a very difficult decision which took a long time for them to make, and after deciding for and against the surgery on and off again, they finally decided to go forward with the surgery. The surgery took several hours but was successful. One of the twins woke up earlier than her sister who remained in the ICU. The mother sat beside the sister who had awakened as they chatted and talked of how grateful they were about the outcome. The mother gently told her daughter that she would be back in a few minutes after getting her some ice chips. Just as the mother left the room, her daughter began to have an anxiety attack. Her heart was racing, her eyes were wide open as she looked over the lonely space which she had never experienced before. She began to shake and shiver, and it seems as if the quietness in the room began to come alive as noise. Just as she felt to cry out for her mom, the mother came back through the door and comforted her and it was then that she too realized that this was a new experience for her, and not a nice one. She had a constant companion, not only by her side, but literally connected at the head; more intimate that most would feel comfortable with; however this of course, came with no options.

    Christ, our Redeemer knows all too well the experience of being alone in a space without the one who has been beside Him for all of eternity. These same anxious emotions griped Him as He hung upon the cross paying the penalty for you and me. One could wonder why he would call out to his Father, "Why have you forsaken me?" Well, He felt so ever keenly, the coldness, the rejection, the harsh and cruel pain of the consequence of sin as He received the punishment in our stead. The separation from His Father was worse than any lashing, or physical pain He could have experienced.

Because He knows the awful feeling of being all alone, it is the very reason Jesus has made it His business to make sure that we know He will never allow us to feel that deep sense of loss and loneliness. That is why, in His compassion, it is so important to Jesus today, to comfort us and remind us that He has promised to never, never leave us alone. So when you are in a space you may have never felt before and you feel alone, like no one cares, know that you are not alone, Jesus is right there, pick up His word right then and read it. Just believe it and claim His promises.

You are NOT alone!

"I Thought You Knew"

I thought you knew I was hanging on
by a thread,
All mixed up in my head.
Down trodden and ashamed of how life dealt me
a raw game.
I thought you knew that meeting you played a
role in saving my ole sole
I thought you knew that one day I'm up and
another day I'm down.
Sometimes my emotions would go around
and around.
Truly, I thought you knew
Life can be hurtful to the core...
I sit in my bed crying all night behind
closed doors.
But the real hurt stems from the fact that...
I thought you knew
Knew that I had just about given up. Hiding my
gutted-out feelings of pain.
Ready to step off the scene, while acting all mean
I thought you knew
That it was people like YOU who said the right
thing at the right time
Saving me as I walked a thin line.

*Life has kicked me up and down the road of
hard knocks
Made me worse, than someone on the rocks, but
I thought you knew
How can it hurt so bad? Because I thought you
knew that I was sad.
That some days it took all I had within me to
face the day, to get out of bed
Depression, anger, and sadness hanging
over my head.
The safest place seemed to be in my bed, but, I
thought you knew
That the crowd was the loneliest place for me,
but the time
We spend one-on-one is the remedy.
I thought you knew
I was coming back from a battle I almost lost,
almost defeated by low self-worth, compromised
dignity and lack of pride.
Finally realizing I can come out and can be
counted as good as any one,
Not having to hide,
But….
I thought you knew
That my struggle with the twins who abide
within is sometimes greater than I can bear, but
by God's grace,
I push forward, I dare*

*I am only damaged goods, crying out for help,
looking for love.
My talk is big, but without power, only yap, yap,
yap, every hour.
I thought you knew
I didn't care enough about me to take care to be
free and that I needed
People who care to stamp a seal of
approval on me
To love me so I could blossom and grow...but I
guess you didn't know.*

Romans 7:24-25

"Oh unhappy and pitiable and wretched man that I am! Who will release and deliver me from this body of death?

"Oh thank God, through Jesus Christ our Lord."

According to the Meridian-Webster dictionary, the definition of Depression is: Feelings of severe despondency and dejection. And according to NIMH- National Institute of Mental Health: Depression is a common but serious mood disorder. It causes severe symptoms that affect how you feel, think, and handle daily activities, such as sleeping, eating or working."

Depression and sadness, feelings of despair, loneliness, and anger are all tactics that the enemy uses time and again to push us into the abyss of a hopeful, point of no return. According to ADA Anxiety and Depression Association of America states that a form of depression; Persistent depressive disorder or PDD, affects approximately 1.5 per cent of the U.S population, age 18 and older, in a given year. (3.3 million American adults).

Paul speaks of this same miserable shackle of oppression as he often spoke of the struggle with the "inner man". But he proclaims the answer to the problem- Jesus Christ our Lord.

Chances are you are one of the many millions of people affected by this thing called depression and all of its associated partners in crime. The anger, which is an emotion closely related to and many times exchanged for pain. Anger, is said to be most easily handled as people are less likely to tolerate pain but feel that with choosing anger, they are in more control. The truth is in the pudding, how many times have you seen a person exploding and totally out of control as his or her anger has reached an uncontrollable limit? At this point, people are injured, families are torn apart; hearts are broken. Don't be that person!

We have all experienced some level of these emotions from time to time, but to have an onslaught of them that seem to rule our lives for long periods of time is not good. One should seek help from a source that will provide a stable emotional condition.

Perhaps, a good place to start may be to start with Paul's example, the word of God. The bible says in Hebrews 4:12 that "The Word of God is quick and powerful, sharper than any two -edged sword, piercing to the dividing asunder of soul and spirit, and of the joints and marrow, and is a discerner of thoughts and the intents of the heart." Paul realized he had a battle within that he could not handle and looked to the Lord for help.

Take time with the Word. Jesus is noted in the book of John as being the Word; "and the Word was made flesh, and dwelt among us, (and we beheld his glory, the glory as of the only begotten of the Father,) full of grace and truth." The bible is the love letter that the Word speaks to you and me. Spend time reading that love letter and coming to know the Redeemer, Relentless Lover, Lord, Savior, Confidant and Friend. Jesus loves you and wants the best for you and is the answer to whatever is wrong in your life. But don't be too proud to ask for Clinical help if you feel that things are getting out of control. There is no shame in using all of the resources that the Lord has placed in your path for true healing.

Index

Abuse: 29-32, 86, 88,131-134,135-137,148-152, 170,178-179
Addiction: 36, 131-134,148-152, 166
Angels: 111-113
Beauty: 135,172
Burdens: 148-152, 166, 169, 178, 183
Calm: 135, 141-142, 180
Celebration: 95,109, 155-158, 167, 169, 172
Confidence: 92-94, 95, 108, 117, 131, 167,169, 172
Contentment: 96, 117, 141, 167, 169, 172
Danger: 131-134, 148-152
Depression: 7,143-147,166, 183-187
Denial: 5-7, 23, 73
Divorce: 5-8
Encouragement: 92, 95,101,117, 135-137,167,169,172, 180-182
Empowerment: 117, 175-177, 98, 131, 167, 168,169, 172
Faith: 103-105, 168, 169, 172
Fear: 9,131-134, 141-142, 148-152, 168
Forgiveness: 23, 73, 88,118-119
Freedom: 126-130,131, 164, 166,167,169,172,175
Free Writes: 161
Generosity: 120
Grace: 111, 135
Gratitude: 108-110, 167, 172
Happiness: 95,123,167,172
Health/Healing: 138-140, 169, 172
Holy Spirit: 43, 46, 116, 176

Hope: 106-107, 111, 126, 135, 141, 143, 168, 169, 172, 180
Honor: 75-78, 155-160
Insecurity: 106, 121, 126-130, 167, 169, 183
Love: 14-15, 64-67, 81, 122, 123, 163
Loneliness: 109, 143-147,166, 180-182
Manipulation: 127-130, 148-152,178-179
Mental Health Issues: 51-54, 143-147, 183-185
Miracle: 46
Moving Forward: 116, 126,141,155-160,167, 169, 172
Pain: xviii, 23, 119,121,136-137, 148-152
Power: 98,103,106,108,126-130, 141,167, 169, 172, 186
Praise: 111, 138,167, 168, 172
Prayer: 43-45, 111
Restoration/Redemption/Revival: 81, 123, 172
Reflection: 116, 122, 155-160, 172, 175-177
Relationships: 75-78,116, 122, 148-152, 154-160
Sadness/Sorrow: 166,175,183-186
Shame: 148-151, 183
Self-Discovery/Help: 170, 172
Strength: 108-110, 168, 172,175, 186
Suicide: 46, 143-147
Trials: 101-102,166
Trauma: xxiv, 1, 3-6, 9, 42, 45, 49,138-140,148-152, 170,175
Victory: 98,106,126,141,167,169,172
Wisdom:xxii-xxiii, 98-100, 116

To my UNSUNG HERO: my son JERAL:

You have been there for me through the deep waters of the unknown. I applaud you for hanging with me even when you were too young to really understand what danger you were in.

I was inspired by you as you continued to love, love, love your father. You were there through all of the changes that he and I went through during the hard years of our youth. As we grew to be better parents, better people, with the knowledge of a greater destiny for each of us; you were there.

I am proud of you today for who you have become; a wise and handsome great young man, a wonderful and capable father, and esteemed son to me. It was so encouraging for me to hear you say, "Where is my book?!"

I am so thrilled that you find the things that I write about so interesting! You show such an excitement to get to know more about who I am through my writing.

I would like to apologize to you for all that you had to endure, just being my son and going through that turbulent time in our lives. I love you the more for it.

I pray that this book, will be for you, a greater blessing than for anyone else who will read it, as you, along with God first, have been the wind beneath my wings to get it done.

It is my desire that your heart will be changed for the better and you will grow and share all that was good when you reviewed it.

May God continue to bless you with health and strength, wealth and wisdom, and the grace to accomplish your heart felt desired goals and to be that clay that He may use to His glory every day that you exist.

Sincerely, with all my love,
Mom

To my Personal Counselor, My dear daughter Moriah:

What would I have done without you? I cannot say. You were there for me in bigger ways than the law allows; but you held your own and developed into a nice mature, hands-on Counselor with wits much beyond your years. Unfortunately, yet very fortunately, you were there during the times when the results of all the abuse that I had to endure yielded its mental and emotional affects. God, nevertheless, must have given you a sense of intuition, strength, and the ability to read human kind from afar.

I thank you for being there for me, really for us. Together we were a good team that, by God's grace, beat the odds.

You are a special person designed with a special kind of foresight and compassion for the underdog. This is your calling for those who you will meet along the way. I am certain that this is why God has placed such a beautiful set of lungs within you; so that you can lay a large platform so that His graces to humanity can be seen, felt, and heard. I look forward to seeing what He has planned in particular with the voice that causes people to cry.

May God continue to bless your path as you live for Him and share your great sense of being able to spot the enemy at the on- set. This saved the day!

Sincerely, with all my love,
Mom

Resources

National Sexual Violence Resource Center
www.nsvrc.org
877-739-3895

National Helpline/SAMHSA-Substance Abuse and Mental Health
www.samhsa.gov
1-800-662-HELP (4357)

National Victims Center
80-FYI-CALL
1-800-394-2255

National Domestic Violence Hotline
www.thehotline.org
800799-7233, 800-787-3224

National Council on Child Abuse and Family Violence Helpline
800-222-2000

National Coalition Against Domestic Violence
www.ncadv.org/need-support/what-is-domestic-violence

Mental Health infosource- 1-800-447-4474

National Association for Children of Alcoholics-1-888-554-2627

National Suicide Prevention Lifeline – 1800-273-TALK

Narcotic Anonymous- http://www.na.org-1-800-342-3487

Are You Broken? You Can Be Restored!

Adolescent Crisis Intervention and Counseling Nineline: 1-800-999-9999

Homeless/Runaway Hotline: 1-800-runaway

1-800-SUICIDE- 1-800-273-TALK

Thank you for the purchase of this book. I hope that you will get out of it as much as I have put into it, and that your life will be enhanced because of reading it.

Please look forward to my next book.

May God continue to bless you as you share his goodness with others.

Sincerely,
Jill Kennedy

For public speaking engagements please call 912-228-0829

CPSIA information can be obtained
at www.ICGtesting.com
Printed in the USA
LVHW021705161218
600532LV00009B/66/P